ONCE UPON A DREAM

Berkshire Bards

Edited By Allie Jones

First published in Great Britain in 2017 by:

YoungWriters Est. 1991

Young Writers
Coltsfoot Drive
Peterborough
PE2 9BF
Telephone: 01733 890066
Website: www.youngwriters.co.uk

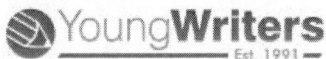

FOREWORD

Welcome to 'Once Upon A Dream - Berkshire Bards'.

For our 'Once Upon A Dream' competition, we invited primary school pupils to delve within their deepest imaginations and create poetry inspired by dreams. They were not limited to the dreams they experience during their sleep, they were free to explore and describe their dreams and aspirations for the future, what could inspire a dream, and also the darker side of dreams... the nightmare!

The topic proved to be hugely popular, with children dreaming up the cleverest, craziest and, sometimes, creepiest of poems! The entries we received showcase the writing talent and inspired imaginations of today's budding young writers.

Congratulations to Quan Nguyen, who has been selected as the best poet in this anthology, hopefully this is a dream come true! Also a big well done to everyone whose work is included within these pages, I hope seeing it published help you continue living your writing dreams!

Allie Jones

CONTENTS

Lola O'Neill (8) 76
Lily Jane Mansell (8) 77
Tyler Chaplin (8) 78
Ethan Duggin (8) 79
Emma Kemp (8) 80
Helena Jewell (9) 81
Laila Rose Frank-Gore (8) 82
Mia Perillo (8) 83
Leon Charles Frank-Gore (8) 84
Anthony Lopez (8) 85
Aaryaa Awasthi (9) 86
Priscilla Abankwa (8) 87
Jude Richard-James Carswell (9) 88
Joshua McCarthy (9) 89
Sienna Mulholland (8) 90

Kennet Valley Primary School, Reading

Karthini Sharma (10) 91
Heidi Lewis (10) 92
Sienna Cluderay (10) 94
Norah Cyril (10) 95
Cody Sanders (10) 96
Naeema Chowdhury (10) 97
Mia Elisa Dell (9) 98
Amber Dixon (9) 99
Avie Alcock (9) 100
Christina Paul (9) 101
Olivia Webb (10) 102
Daniel Birose (10) 103
Kirstie Bates (9) 104
Casper Jennings (9) 105
Jack Robert Bayliss (9) 106

Marish Primary School, Slough

Tanvi Davuluri (11) 107
Zara Amber Khan (11) 108
Hasini Pulavarthi (8) 109
Druti Vasist (11) 110
Natalia Dudek (8) 111
Naomi Nash (11) 112
Isha Pothineni (8) 113

Unique Oluoha (7) 114
Arshiya Gupta (7) 115
Chloe Corcoran (7) 116
Rithvick Dittakavi (10) 117
Bartlomiej Brandys (8) 118
Sam Hopkins (11) 119

Nas Thames Valley School, Reading

Gabriel Alexander Addario-Prado (9) 120
James Sandford (9) 121
Dominic Bell (9) 122
Daniel Van-Asperen (9) 123

Park Lane Primary School, Reading

Maggie Sinani (10) 124
Emily Hall (9) 126
Sreevedha Bhuvaneshwaran (8) 127
Thomas Brooks (10) 128
Leah Whittington (9) 129
Talullah Mae Linger (8) 130
Emilie Homer (10) 131
Emily Watkinson (10) 132
Isabella Charlotte Moon (7) 133
Anya Thomas (9) 134

St Peter's CE Middle School, Windsor

Harry Weston (11) 135
Charlie Drane (11) 136
Shrey Gala (10) 138
McKenzie Hoogers (11) 140
Holly Lewis (10) 142
Elena Mills (11) 144
Lilianna Nhamburo (11) 146
Adam Fodor Sfendla (10) 148
Arjun Bassi (11) 149
Isabelle Brett (10) 150
Jakob Howard-Real (10) 151

Holly Alden (9)	152	
Bo Isabel Sampson (10)	153	
Ewan Moore (11)	154	
Alec Collins (11)	156	
Georgia Van Der Brugge (11)	157	
Millie Edwards (9)	158	
Thomas Sielski (11)	159	
Ellie Breach (10)	160	
John Valdez (10)	161	
Harry O'Shaughnessy (10)	162	
Leonna Nhamburo (11)	163	
Seth Thomson (10)	164	
Obi Ijeomah (10)	165	
Harrison Wingrove (10)	166	
Eloise Hall (10)	167	
Liberty Groves (11)	168	
Oliver Wright (11)	169	
Roxanne Rejnisz (10)	170	
Ben Pleace (10)	171	
Charlotte Roberts (10)	172	
Joshua Ernest Claassen (10)	173	
Amani Mahamud (11)	174	
Jamie Haydock-Wilson (11)	175	
Joshua Williams (10)	176	
Angus Padwick (11)	177	
Yasmina Patricia Tahiri (11)	178	
Katie Beale (11)	179	
Olivia Clark (11)	180	
Madinah Khan (11)	181	
Ellie-Mai Worthington (10)	182	
Jay Stephen Moody (11)	183	
Joshua Gomes (11)	184	
Morgan O'Neill (11)	185	
Ria Martin (10)	186	
Charles Keen (11)	187	
Edith Armfield-Shepherd (11)	188	
Ben Puscy (11)	189	
Brandon McCulley (11)	190	
Grace Williams (10)	191	

Willow Primary School, Slough

Aaliah Malik (10)	192
Kaaynat Anwar (9)	194
Raja Amin Khan (9)	196
Imaan Jalil (9)	197
Muqaddas Kamran (9)	198
Skeena Zara Shah (9)	199
Amirah Zamurad (9)	200

THE POEMS

Well done! Your poem has been chosen as the best in this book.

Defeating Voldemort Didn't Go All Too Well...

I was in a car in a deep, pungent black,
Moving slowly along, past creepy shacks.
I gripped the wand hidden in my pocket
lying impatiently there with Tom Riddle's locket,
which was only a spangled remain,
smouldering rectangles hanging from a chain.

After two hours we reached Ufton Court,
where we were told we would find Voldemort.
We searched and searched, searched and searched
for our guide, a real-life talking bird!

We finally found him in the darkening wood
'Be quick!' he said. 'Run as fast as you could!
You'll find Voldemort on a big, wrecked hill.
Stop him now or someone will be tortured and killed...'

And sure enough, up there on the hill
Stood Voldemort so menacingly still,
With the speeding of my heartbeat, I just knew
The only way to stop him was to duel.

So with a swipe of our wands, we began to fight
The whole courtyard was glowing with light

Avada Kedavra!
Bang!

With the light fading from my eyes,
I knew the deadly Killing Curse must have struck.
Voldemort had won - it was just not my luck...

I sat bolt upright and looked at my mirror
Scanned it once and saw the noseless terror...
Avada Kedavra!

Quan Nguyen (9)
Geoffrey Field Junior School, Reading

The Unicorn And Me

T he sky was full of enchantment
H e was all alone and his neck was bent
E nding the day was like when you run out of chocolate

U nicorns would hug their mascot, Piglet
N ow the day had just begun
I 'm now a unicorn rider, so the fun had just begun
C ome and stay, we'll play all day
O r the unicorn could well stay till the end of May
R un around, let's make a sound
N ow we are above the ground

A nd we'll scream and shout
N ow will let it all out
D on't hurt yourself

M any people did and turned into an elf
E nding May was not a special day not a single one of us left at the last day.

Jasmine Patricia Elizabeth Anne Fairchild (11)
Chaddleworth St Andrew's & Shefford CE Federated Primary Schools, Hungerford

The Unicorn

I had a dream last night
A unicorn appeared
It took me on a journey
To another atmosphere
It took me to a woodland
Of colours I've never seen
A little land of beauty
With a little running stream
The sky was alight with glory
The water a piercing blue
A feeling of excitement
How could this be true?

Maybe in my mind I built this perfect place
A place of great excitement
But this is not the case
This amazing place is real
The unicorn told me so
I'm here to spend the rest of my life
On a dream I can't let go
Over a rainbow we flew and into a portal of light
The grass was so green
Oh what a lovely scene

So happy we seemed always together
There's no end to my dream
It goes on forever.

Ella Mundy (10)
Geoffrey Field Junior School, Reading

Olympic Dreams

O lympic gold medals are waiting for me
L eotards and scrunchies so very shiny
Y ouTube videos showed me where to start
M otivation was all I needed in my heart
P ikes, straddles and splits is where it began
I know that this is all part of my plan
C onditioning and stretching to help me get strong

D reaming and believing that this is where I belong
R ed and black are the colours of my team
E ven though I may fall I will not give up my dream
A ll the training I do tomorrow and today
M y strong need to win shows me the way
S tarlings in Bracknell is where the new years begins.

You can do it
Win, win, win.

Ella Main (8)
Geoffrey Field Junior School, Reading

What A Day!

A huge audience happily cheers
With my family in joyful tears
My heart started beating very fast
Then the lights came on at last
Surprisingly the queen came to stay
I just didn't know what to say
I strode upon the stage in London
As sweat trickled down my cheek
I sang the most beautiful song
It lasted for long and long
I couldn't stop the wonderful feeling
It made the inside of my heart to glow
Everybody clapped to the beat
Taking their bottoms out of their seats
A confident smile came to my face
I think it's time to keep up the pace
We danced happily under the night sky
I felt that I was going to cry.

Priyanka Raj (8)
Geoffrey Field Junior School, Reading

My Dream

My exciting journey begins
With the magic of the wind
I go to sleep, shut my eyes
And my dream begins to rise

I'm with a giant meerkat
I pop on my hat
We fly away high
Into the sky

'It's chilly up here,'
The meerkat fears
'Put on a coat,'
As we went down in a slope

The lollipop trees
In the woods are set free
I sit on a sofa
And feel a bit closer

They are marshmallow
And I'm glad they're yellow
Suddenly a man appears
Oh no, he was already here

He gave me a present
Wrapped very pleasant
It was a Rubix cube
And some stew.

Megan Allen (8)
Geoffrey Field Junior School, Reading

Dreams

Dreams are complex and beautiful things
You can have good ones or dark scary nightmares.

Good dreams are joyful, peaceful and fun
But nightmares completely block out the sun.

But what is a nightmare? I hear you sigh
Well, all I can tell you is that it'll make you cry!

Now let's get back to good dreams
Some of them are so nice you'll never want to leave!
They can be set on a riverbank or on a
bright summer's day
Where all the characters have kind things to say.

You get them when you're asleep
So you might want to rush
Go to your bed, cuddle up and hush...

Wallaree Snehal Vaishampayan (9)
Geoffrey Field Junior School, Reading

What Happens In My Head

Jar upon jar
Row upon row
Bar upon bar
Of memory, nightmares and dreams

Trolls and gods
Ships and cards
Nether wart and blaze rods
These are flashes of memory

Paper and pen
River of light
Dog and hen
These are flashes of dreams

Dark forest
Creepy clown
Deer eating wolf all around
These are flashes of nightmares

The dreams are like beacons
In a fog
Memories are old milestones
Nightmares are bars of lead
Most of these happen to me
When I'm in bed.

Eoghan Herriott (9)
Geoffrey Field Junior School, Reading

Haunted House

Strange things happened last night
I woke up, there was no light
I looked carefully around
I could hear a creaking sound
Behind a corner I caught a glimpse of a little glow
Somebody tiptoed, I moved really slow
In here is like a haunted house
Maybe there is a squeaky mouse
I feel like I'm a tortoise in my shell
I think that there's a witch casting a spell
Downstairs I found a clue
I walked back upstairs then, 'Boo!'
Now I really woke up
No, it wasn't my pup
It was my friend
And that is the end.

Miriam Baroud (8)
Geoffrey Field Junior School, Reading

A Dream For Everyone

A dream for everyone
Everyone screams for help
Only in a nightmare
But my story is different
It's about a fantasy world which is
All locked and barred.

I wander there to find out
where the key is hidden
I can see good people
Playing in the sweet world
My dear unicorn was desperate to go in

The keys were behind a prickly bush
But I knew I'll get better in fantasy world
I reached out, I got it
I walked, I unlocked, I went in
And finally I stayed full of sweets.

Hajira Azam (9)
Geoffrey Field Junior School, Reading

Dreamworld

Dreamworld, Dreamworld
Where can I go?
Dreamworld, Dreamworld
In a land of snow.

Dreamworld, Dreamworld
Wonder where you are
Dreamworld, Dreamworld
Right next to a star.

Dreamworld, Dreamworld
Who are you?
Dreamworld, Dreamworld
I am Winnie the Pooh.

Dreamworld, Dreamworld
What can I do?
Dreamworld, Dreamworld
Let's go to the zoo.

Dreamworld, Dreamworld
How do you feel?
Dreamworld, Dreamworld
As happy as can be.

Lansana Sheku Mansaray (9)
Geoffrey Field Junior School, Reading

A Boat Journey

The sea glistened in the moonlight like a magical spell
The wind pushed the boat like an engine
The sea allowed the boat to pass as if the police was passing
The sails gently flapped against the wind
The birds gradually glided through the dark sky.

All was peaceful and calm
Nothing could do any harm
The large boat sailed further
But then I heard a *crack!*
Swoosh!
Suddenly the boat got lower... and lower and lower
At that moment, I found myself in bed.

Jakub Pazderski (9)
Geoffrey Field Junior School, Reading

Mist-Ery

When I close my eyes
And I'm tucked up safe in bed
If I'm for a nightmare
My eyelids will glow red

If the worst should happen
Next will come the mist
Fog as thick and dense
As a boxer's punching fist

The lack of sound is eerie
My heart is filled with dread
I know the awful image
Soon will haunt my head

The picture is so terrible
My mind begins to fizz
But as soon as I awake
I can't remember what it is...

Annabelle Tarr (9)
Geoffrey Field Junior School, Reading

My Dream

In Dream Land far away with a unicorn
Where the grass is yellow
The paths were purple
And the sky is orange

There is a house filled with dream pots
Made of delicious lollipop trees
Crumbly gingerbread doors
And wobbly jelly windows

But *drip!* While I was inside
A dreampot split
Bang! went the power
The dream was as colourful as a parachute

The dream made us fly, weeeee!
And my dream didn't stop!

Emily Allen (10)
Geoffrey Field Junior School, Reading

The Nightmare Of Moving Country

The house was empty
The car was on
The aeroplane was booked but nothing was done
I still had time but
My new house was clean, empty and vacuumed
My mum was ready
My dad was steady
The car was roaring to go
My mum dragged me in the car
My dad pulled me in the aeroplane
I was asleep I ended, I don't know where
The next minute I woke up and my mum
said, 'Let's go...'

Zaynah Chaudhry (8)
Geoffrey Field Junior School, Reading

In A Faraway Land

In a faraway land
We went to explore
And here's what we saw

Some purple mist
A fairy's list
A flying dog
A magical log
A racing cat
A zooming mat
A tiny unicorn
And a phoenix being born
Some floating bubbles
And rabbit couples
Some very strange echoes
And flying geckos

This is what we found
Oh and an angel in the lounge.

Madeline Kamara (9)
Geoffrey Field Junior School, Reading

Floating In The Sky

In the moonlight sky
Two children sat
Staring at the stars
Sending them into Dreamland
They dreamt of
Puffy, soft clouds
With the two cheeky children
Almost tasting it
It was pink, it was delicious, it was cotton candy
They dreamt of
Fun with their families on a beautiful, summer day.

Out of Dreamland, feeling amazing, magical
Anything could happen to them.

Eva Kasia Lee (9)
Geoffrey Field Junior School, Reading

Unicorns

U sually you don't find unicorns very much

N obody has ever seen one this close

I did last night, so near I could touch

C ould see her sparkling eyes and glittering nose

O ver the night sky she flies like a bird

R ainbow trail behind wherever she goes

N ow I have to wait until bedtime to see her again, waiting silently without breathing a word.

Elouize Grace Goswell-Janes (8)
Geoffrey Field Junior School, Reading

Famous Dancer

F lying through the air
A crobatics too
M oving to the beat
O h how fun it can be
U p on stage we go
S uper dancing.

D ancing is so fun
A nother competition
N ine out of ten, the points that I score
C ompetitions are fun
E very move counts
R acing to go on stage.

Marley Victoria Anne Niole (8)
Geoffrey Field Junior School, Reading

If I Had Powers

If I had powers, if I had powers, if I had powers
Magical, wonderful, sparkling powers
Colossal, shining, beautiful powers
If I had powers, if I had powers, if I had powers.

If I had powers, if I had powers, if I had powers
Amazing, aqua, multicoloured powers
Tremendous, fire or ice, changing powers
If I had powers, if I had powers, if I had powers.

Freya-Sky Thomas (9)
Geoffrey Field Junior School, Reading

Starlight

Starlight, starlight, what a wonderful night
I gaze around and have a fright
Fairy light, starlight, starlight, what a wonderful night
It was the tooth fairy
The teeth-stealer
Coin-giver
Fast-flyer
Dust-dropper
Teeth-collector
Message-receiver
Starlight, starlight, you made my heart light
I love starlight.

Bavleen Kaur Kamna (8)
Geoffrey Field Junior School, Reading

So High Up

I was in bed fast asleep
I heard a weird beep
It was no ordinary sound
Also, I found myself not on the ground
I hid under my pillow
Under me was a willow
I screamed out loud
But nobody heard me because I was on a cloud
I went near a plane
The man from the plane sent a crane
I was down
Safe and sound.

Maximilien Autié (8)
Geoffrey Field Junior School, Reading

Luna

Soaring through the sky
In my land
Here I fly
No dragon banned

I see...
Dragon fights
Eggs hatching
Dragon flights
Fish catching

As I fly down town
All heads down

For I am Luna, the seadragon, gigantic
Maximus the dragon ruler!

Lisa Norgate (9)
Geoffrey Field Junior School, Reading

I Dream To Be A Dancer

When I grow up I dream to be a dancer
Dancing for cheers, dancing for laughter
Doing groovy moves such as pop and lock
And maybe Scooby-Doo, helicopter, Bart Simpson
And many more I could do after
So when I grow up I dream to be a dancer
Dancing for cheers, dancing for laughter.

Amara Jumpp (10)
Geoffrey Field Junior School, Reading

In My World

I can see chocolate river flowing up and down...
Gingerbread house running about...
I can see candy people laughing about...
I can taste sweet candyfloss in my mouth...
I'm running in the air like reindeer
Looking down at my world
Wondering what will be next.

Nimrah Raja (10)
Geoffrey Field Junior School, Reading

Unicorns

U p in the clouds the unicorns fly
N obody can see them except from I
I want to be one of them
C onquering the clouds
O ccasionally popping their head out of the sky
R eally just to say hi
N obody can see them but I.

Jack Bennett (10)
Geoffrey Field Junior School, Reading

Sunset

S himmering sunset in the sky
U nited Kingdom have a good night
N ight, night my pretty, see you tomorrow
S himmering sunset in the sky
E very sunset is so pretty
T ommy, Dad, Mum, Bruno and Jesus have a good night.

Lillee Godwin (9)
Geoffrey Field Junior School, Reading

Unicorns

Unicorns, unicorns, have rainbow hair
With magnificent wings gliding through the air
Unicorns, unicorns, have clippy-cloppy hooves
Which sparkle in the sun as they move
Unicorns, unicorns, have a shiny horn
That flashes at the darkness of dawn.

Ruby Allen (9)
Geoffrey Field Junior School, Reading

My Great Dream

I will put in my dream...
The gushing river rapidly rippling down the mountain in
front of my eyes
The amazing feeling of riding on the back of a unicorn
galloping valiantly
Of me walking across a bridge of strawberry laces
The rush of being the pilot flying an aeroplane through
the powder-blue sky
Seeing a mighty lion racing proudly at a speedy pace

I will put in my dream...
Sitting on the beach as golden as the shining
glimmering sun
To hear the pleased crowd screaming my name
at the Oscars
I would also love to eat colourful candyfloss
until there's none
And definitely to meet my godfather in Heaven
one more time

I will put in my dream...
To see the stony walls of Buckingham Palace one day
I'd love to swim in a chocolate river meandering rapidly
To hear a horse loudly and proudly say, 'Nay!'

I will put in my dream...
To witness Neverland with my own eyes
One day for somebody to end wars
I wish I would never have to say my goodbyes
My dream is to explore another galaxy in a
mighty rocket ship

I will put in my dream...
Myself posing at the end of a long scarlet carpet
years from now
To see the amazing white house for myself
I'd like to feed a flying cow but just how
But the thing is, dreams do come true!

Lily Moran (8)
Jennett's Park CE Primary School, Bracknell

My Life... Dreams...

I will start off to put into my dream...
A mouth-watering world of candy
And scrumdiliumptious gummy bears
And scrumptious whipped cream
And sticky candyfloss.
And scrummy, yummy, drizzling...Nutella!

I will next put into my dream...
Me modelling down a long, silk, red ruby carpet
With all my fans taking particularly
bright flashing pictures.

I will then put into my dream...
An extremely humungous, evil... burger!
Trying to destroy the world with an army of
chips and nuggets.
Boom!

I will put into my dream...
Me running with a courageous, cunning, brave and
wild Wolf Blood
With yellow glowing eyes and veiny black veins
And razor-sharp teeth, black claws and fluffy white fur.

I will put into my dream...
Me in a famous gymnast dance studio

Showing off all my dance skills
As a beautiful, professional dancer.

Finally, I will put into my dream...
Beautifully patterned snowflakes falling from
the heavens above
Into a deep heap of snow.
Until the sun gives a blazing, beaming smile
Like an extremely happy child!

Alessia Utting (8)
Jennett's Park CE Primary School, Bracknell

The Magical Land

I will start my dream with...
The BFG, Danielle, Jamie and Ethan playing a football
match against evil villains including the evil giants
The head of the good team is BFG and for the
bad team, Bonecruncher

I will put into my dream...
Silly snapping burgers, chicken nuggets and chips that
try to eat the world
Thankfully we figured out that we could just
eat the food
Danielle took the mouth-watering burger, Jamie took
the scrumptious chicken nuggets and Ethan took
the epic chips

I will put into my dream...
Harley Quinn, Joker, Spider-Man and Spider Girl
We changed Harley Quinn and Joker to be good so
they will not be bad again or annoying to
goodies like Batman

I will put into my dream...
Jojo in Bow Land where there are pools made of bows
and we sing like angels singing peaceful opera with
an echoing *boom!*

I will put into my dream...
Danielle walking down the ruby-red carpet in New York
with a shimmering long turquoise dress on

I will finish my dream...
Bows jumping joyfully, the evil giants smiled, the whole
Earth is peaceful.

Danielle Dickinson (9)
Jennett's Park CE Primary School, Bracknell

The Magical Dream

I will put into my dream
Going back in time, *tick, tick, tick*
The one time touching the stars with the tip of
my thinger ding
Going to the future, *ch, ch, ch*

I will put into my dream
A whoosh from a rainbow slide
A flying unicorn that goes, *clip-clop, clip-clop*
Air from a rocket going everywhere

I will put into my dream
A world of smiggle, *mmm*
Being able to fly with wings as big as two metres
Also to be able to be invisible when I click my fingers

I will put into my dream
Finding a mythical land
Having a castle as my house
Have servants tidy my house

My dream will be fashioned from
Fluffy marshmallows that cover my land of
dreams around me
My favourite pictures are for my ground in the
Land of Dreams

I will float into my dream
Without pixie dust just like Peter Pan
And all the dreams will be in a different door
And I can just float into my favourite ones when I want.

Honey Lee (8)
Jennett's Park CE Primary School, Bracknell

The Magic Dream

I will put into my dream
The magical wand of Hermione Granger
Swooshes of a mermaid's gliding tail
Elusive T-rex bones

I will put into my dream
The thrill of being in a Spitfire's cockpit
The unmistakable taste of a gingerbread house
Hissing sounds of Lord Voldemort's snake

I will put into my dream
A squealing princess being kidnapped
The velvet mane of a soaring alicorn
The adventure of running Willy Wonka's factory

I will put into my dream
The hilt of the queen's knighting sword
A child's first sighting of a smiling sunset
A caramel lake lying in relaxation

My dream will be fashioned from
Pure gold, sugar and flames
With a rainbow surrounding it
Its hinges are oiled with the purest water

I will dive into my dream
On a bouyancy aid of candyfloss
Then wrap myself in a towel of clouds
As soft as a mattress.

Isla Price (9)

Jennett's Park CE Primary School, Bracknell

The Magic Dream

I will put into my dream
The nib of a pen scratching on the paper
The first spell cast by a wizard
Turning small and having an adventure on
the table top

I will put into my dream
The sound of a dolphin's chattering teeth
Grinning bubbles floating out of a gushing waterfall
The dinosaurs' last glance before being lost forever

I will put into my dream
The day of training a petrifying dragon
Fallen feathers of a bird
Glistening froth of a whirlpool

I will put into my dream
The first rainbow to appear on Earth
A ride on a phoenix
Chocolate swimming pools smiling grandly

My dream will be fashioned from
The stars of outer space
The golden sun's beaming smile
The Milky Way galaxy

I will clamber into my dream
Then somersault as swiftly as an eagle
through my dream
Into a candy cloud and land with a *bang!*

Viyath Wanninayake (9)
Jennett's Park CE Primary School, Bracknell

The Magic Dream

I will put into my dream...
Soft, splashing sounds of mermaids
The voice of a princess as sweet as a bird
And the sound of a machine going to the future, *bang!*

I will put into my dream...
A colourful rainbow slide
Marshmallow beds as soft as cotton
And whoosh up in the sky with a unicorn

I will put into my dream...
A mansion of lollipops, *mmm*
The sound of a dolphin calling
A pet turtle as slow as a snail.

I will put into my dream...
Snow dancing gracefully in the air
A chocolate fountain as big as Big Ben
And the crackling sound of me going back in time

My dream will be fashioned by
Glistening ice that shone in the sun
Crystals as pointy as a sharp knife
And diamonds as shiny as can be

I will float into my dream
On a beautiful horse
As white as snow
With skin very warm.

Amaya White (8)
Jennett's Park CE Primary School, Bracknell

My Lovely Dream

I will put into my dream...
Walking slowly on the scarlet carpet
Being rich and famous
And being a raging sprinter in the Olympics

I will put into my dream...
Being in a peaceful candy (with chocolate) world
With candy unicorns soaring above me
And a milk chocolate waterfall

I will put into my dream...
A multicoloured rainbow in the very distance
A place of cheerful comedy
And grins on people's faces as they quickly walk by

I will put into my dream...
Happy moments from the past
My job in the brilliant future
And my caring family

I will put into my dream...
Buttercups and daisies swaying in the breeze
Soft teddies smiling at you
And happy weather around beautiful Earth

I will put into my dream...
Going on an adventure with a famous person
Having a lovely life
And munching on custard creams!

Josh William Eggington (8)
Jennett's Park CE Primary School, Bracknell

The Magic Dream

I will put into my dream
The flowing water of the Great Barrier Reef
Living on a tropical mythical island in the shape
of a Pegasus
And the whoosh of going to outer space

I will put into my dream
Living in a flying candy house
Being able to hear the flowing water of the
East Australian Current
To discover the end of the world that is as blue
as the sky

I will put into my dream
Having a pet doughnut and a chocolate chip
candyfloss cookie
I want to become queen of the underwater world
I would love to bottle tonnes of stardust

I will put into my dream
Having a pet Alicorn
To become a world-known author
Or to be a famous artist

My dream is fashioned from
candyfloss clouds

And cookie thoughts and dreams
Made of ice cream

I shall leap into my dream
On chocolate buttons
That melt as you step on them.

Hannah Drablow (9)
Jennett's Park CE Primary School, Bracknell

The Weird Wonderful!

I will put into my dream...
A land full of mouth-watering Candy
All the people will be gummy bears,
And the lakes will be scrumptious melted chocolate,

I will put into my dream...
Going to the amazing Olympics,
And to win a gold, smiling medal
and the people will say, 'Hooray!'

I will put into my dream...
A world that I could rub out
So if there was a dangerous fight I could rub it out
And the world will be at peace again,

I will put into my dream...
To turn around in the dream
So if you are afraid of something
Turn around and face it,

I will not put into my dream...
A world of evil and darkness
or a bee that is hopeless in a garden full
of dead flowers,

I will not put into my dream...
Horrible people that don't listen
Or show the rainbow promise
I will not put into my dream.

Tahlia Williams (9)
Jennett's Park CE Primary School, Bracknell

The Magic Dream

I will put into my dream
Bozena riding on a unicorn flying gracefully in the sky
like a fairy,
A snowman with a rumbling tummy,
An ice palace with a frosty swimming pool,
Owls fluttering in the sky.

I will put into my dream
The first laugh of a baby,
A cowboy on a broomstick,
A witch on a horse,
My first tooth that fell out.

I will put into my dream
A child fast asleep in bed,
A gymnast in the Olympics,
A helpful unicorn laying on the soft, fluffy clouds.

I will put into my dream
A child sitting on ice,
A fairy dancing on ice,
A shimmering waterfall.

I will put into my dream
A red carpet flying in the air,
A book character coming to life.

I will put into my dream
A world made of candyfloss,
The noise of my sister banging the door;
The gift of love.

Bozena Anne Jaasi (8)
Jennett's Park CE Primary School, Bracknell

The Magic Dream

I will put in my dream
Unicorns galloping across the land
A rainbow leaping from world to world
Giant blooming flowers scraping space

I will put in my dream
Majestic mermaids gliding gracefully through the water
Delicate dolphins jumping like a grasshopper
Seaweed tickling fish's fins

I will put in my dream
Fairies fluttering like precious antiques
Bright pink candyfloss trees pointing up to the sky
A mystical garden whispering secrets

I will put in my dream
Snowflakes spiralling down to the ground
Adorable polar bears roaming a land of ice and snow
A block of ice from an abandoned igloo

My dream will be fashioned from
The rays of the smiling sun
Fairy dust scattered around the edge
I will fly in my dream
Over the wondrous landscape
And I would live up in the clouds.

Claudia Lloyd (9)
Jennett's Park CE Primary School, Bracknell

The Dream Jar

I will put into my dream...
A mind-blowing trip to the future in a never
before seen spaceship
Myself standing on the ruby-red carpet in a sparkly
frock holding a golden Grammy award trophy

I will put into my dream...
A life-changing trip to the Olympics to become a
gold medallist swimmer
A relaxing trip to New York City and go see all of
the famous architects

I will put into my dream...
A new adventure to a land where it is all peaceful and
you can ride glittery unicorns with rainbow manes and
a shiny, golden horn

I will ride into my dream...
On a colourful rainbow slide that never ends

I will swim into my dream...
In the salty sea that sways like grass

I will put into my dream...
Me sipping Coca-Cola in LA like a princess, with the
smiling sun.

Katie Page (9)
Jennett's Park CE Primary School, Bracknell

Dream World!

I will put into my dream...
An amazing experience with Darcey Bussell
A wonderful play with a soft and fluffy monster
Thousands of beautiful dresses covering the whole land

I will put into my dream...
Superb sighting of New York
The crash of the waves as I surf across
The sighting of Hermione was as magical as a wizard

I will put into my dream...
A magical sweet land where sweets just fall
from the sky
A swish of Jojo Siwa's famous hair
Colourful talking giraffes

I will put into my dream...
A pink, sparkling, flying unicorn
Rainbow emojis
Smiggel

I will put into my dream...
Matilda coming alive
Walking down the red carpet
Being a famous ballerina

I will put into my dream...
Lots of love
High heel heaven
And a fantastic castle!

Erin Grand (9)
Jennett's Park CE Primary School, Bracknell

The Magic Dream

I will put into my dream
The galloping of a magical unicorn
Plopping of the shimmery fish
The dancing of the glitter onto the colourful rainbow

I will put into my dream
The amazing school on Earth
Flying over the city as shooting star
Owls swooping through the bushes

I will put into my dream
The shiny butterfly flying in the sky
Flying through the candyfloss clouds
Sliding down a rainbow

I will put in my dream
The shiny trolls digging under ground
The shimmering of the mermaid's tail
The bee stinging people

I will fashion my dream from
Chocolate, fluffy marshmallows
With candyfloss clouds and chocolate cake

I will dive into my dream
Landing on marshmallow clouds
Candyfloss, chocolate cake
Strawberry cake and mint cake.

Jessica Chubb (8)
Jennett's Park CE Primary School, Bracknell

The Wonderful Dream

I will put into my dream
The sparkling smile of the sun
A glimpse of the future
A flight of a unicorn
The gallop of a horse

I will put into my dream
A land of smiles
A mermaid swimming happily
The chomp of a candy house
The light of a star

I will put into my dream
The slurp of a candyfloss window
A cloud to float on
Wings to fly like a bird
The colours of colourful paint

I will put into my dream
The sea to swim in
Chocolate to munch on
A white cloud to sleep softly
The frost from a roof

My dream will be fashioned out of
Flying white marshmallow
Puffy candyfloss trees

I will ride a dolphin in my dream
Then fly gracefully through
The enchanted castle
After I will surf on the rolling waves.

Sophie Maunders (8)
Jennett's Park CE Primary School, Bracknell

The Magic Dream

I will put into my dream
The velvet soft hair of a unicorn
A whoosh of a passing shooting star
The power of flying to an unknown world.

I will put into my dream
The sounds of a happy life
And the wonders of outer space
A ride on a colourful rainbow dinosaur

I will put into my dream
The plop of a raindrop
A gingerbread house with cookies as roof tiles
The whole world made from chocolate

I will put into my dream
A land of yummy sweets
The magic power of Hogwarts
A place where there are no more wars

I will fashion my dream from
Shiny gold like a star
With rainbows scattered across
It had fairy wings fluttering about

I will float into my dream
Washing up in Paradise
The beaming sun with birds singing.

Hannah Lilley (8)
Jennett's Park CE Primary School, Bracknell

My Magical Dream

I will put into my dream...
A world of scrumptious candy with candyfloss clouds
Gummy bears as people and houses made out of all
the candy you would like

I will put into my dream...
An Olympic stadium with all the medals you would like
with them smiling joyfully in your face

I will put into my dream...
A colourful rainbow that everyone can slide down and
land on a fluffy, soft cloud

I will put into my dream...
A magical school with teachers that say, 'Do whatever
you like!' and the funnest of schools ever!

Boom! down goes the board
Crash! goes the tables
Bang! there goes the drinks

I will secretly put into my dream...
A peaceful world that if you ever had an argument you
could just rub it out.

Grace Bull (8)
Jennett's Park CE Primary School, Bracknell

The Flawless Dream

I will put into my dream
The ability to fly
A mermaid tail to roam through the sea
A song to sing so I can practise to be a singer.

I will put into my dream
A candyfloss rainbow to slide down
The sparkly smile of the sun grinning
And the face of the moon shining.

I will put into my dream
The flight of a cloud drifting
The light of the stars sparkling
A glimpse of the future.

I will put into my dream
To smile in a mythical land
Chomp and munch on a cupcake village
The ocean waves to feel free and swim.

My dream will be fashioned from
the brightest stars shimmering
Roses from a meadow fluttering and flying fairies.

I shall jump into my dream
and I will come back out by a marshmallow life buoy.

Amaya-Marie Lowry (9)
Jennett's Park CE Primary School, Bracknell

The Mayhem And Happiness Of Your Dreams

I will put into my dream...
A burger land where they were like sly snakes
Their twisty tongues are made out of
mouth-watering tomatoes
And they had had onion teeth that are poisonous

I will put into my dream...
A death realm that you always die if you go there
instead or birds
There are zombie bats but you can have them as pets

I will put into my dream...
A candy land where Coca-Cola bubbles across the river
And candy canes are 2cm tall but there are 1000
trillion of them

I will put into my dream...
A gem land where gems land in the
beautiful, peaceful sunlight
With excitement and joy in their little hearts

I will put into my dream...
A magical world where there are explosions and
someone ran and *boom!*

Luke Whiteside (8)
Jennett's Park CE Primary School, Bracknell

The Big Dream

I will put into my dream
The hullabaloo of a disturbing jungle
A big group of happiness from the blazing sun
The great friendship of a glimmering rainbow.

I will put into my dream
A tall penguin of a milkman doing a big spill!
A big band of wonderful writers
Flaying trees as beautiful as ever.

I will put into my dream
Little cute kittens saying, 'Miaow'
A great Xbox One cake, made out of butter icing
Playing on the plate

I will put into my dream
The bright night sky
A big gulp
A lovely teacher

I will fashion my dream out of
Dark black, as dark as a dark blue pen
The best green glitter

I will cannonball into my dream like no one has ever
before.

Oscar John Akers (8)
Jennett's Park CE Primary School, Bracknell

Dream Jar

I will put into my dream
Me walking down a red ruby carpet
A trip to New York
Me starring in a five-star film

I will put into my dream
A world of candy with a chocolate river
A world of peace and harmony
An amazing trip to LA

I will put into my dream
Me turning round to face my fear
Book characters coming to life
A robot servant

I will put into my dream
Talking dogs
A smiling moon dancing the night away
A world of roller coasters

I will ride on a slide into my dream
As the sun sparkled and fell to bed
A world of rainbows

I will mind blow my dream
With a trip to the future
A whoosh of a ball from Harry Kane
A trip in to a video game.

Archie James (9)
Jennett's Park CE Primary School, Bracknell

The Dream

I will put into my dream
Myself as Toadette
The spiky shell that whizzes in the air
A pounding super giant

I will put into my dream
A sea with sugar, not salt
A world of Smiggle
Three magical clocks

I will put into my dream
The world of cheering toads
Races where everyone is first
Snow as pure as frosting

I will put into my dream
Unbreaking objects
The world of scent
Even with motorbikes that smell nice

I will fashion my dream from
Dancing kittens, Smiggle stationary
And food that does not rot

I will race in my dream
On a motorbike, *voom!*
In the first place
With my scented outfit.

Emilie Charman (9)
Jennett's Park CE Primary School, Bracknell

The Dream

I will put in my dream...
The whoosh of a passing boomerang hitting Joker in his head
Web shooters shooting electric webs
A Spitfire's roaring engine

I will put in my dream...
The whizz of a time machine
The beating wings of a pterodactyl
Joining a team of famous heroes

I will put in my dream...
People forging lightsabres using power crystals
The first beam in a theme park
The first lead of a pencil

I will put in my dream...
The underwater bubbles
Marvels castle underground
The first footsteps in Atlantis

My dream is fashioned from
An Avro Lancaster bomber
A Concorde's flight
A Messerschmitt
I shall fly into my dream on a Lancaster.

James Cervo (8)
Jennett's Park CE Primary School, Bracknell

My Dream

I will put into my dream...
A wonderful candy land with sweets everywhere
A gingerbread house to sleep in
And yummy gummy bears booming out with laughter

I will put into my dream...
A bright red carpet that I could walk across
and be famous

I will put into my dream...
A cute, soft, fluffy monster that brings you hot
chocolate when it's cold
And ice lollies when it's hot

I will put into my dream...
A golden sun shining in the soft wind

I will put into my dream...
A silver moon shining in the darkness
Making the world peaceful and graceful

I will put into my dream...
A whole buffet of sweets and treats
And you could pick anything out of it

Georgia Shearing (8)
Jennett's Park CE Primary School, Bracknell

The Magic Dream

I will put into my dream
The mythical castle of Hogwarts
The sound of a unicorn galloping, *clip-clop*
Turn into a mermaid in an underwater land

I will put into my dream
To have a world of smiggle
Turn into a princess
Watch a shooting star, *whoosh!*

I will put into my dream
The amazing future
Dancing show every day
Live in a place of mythical creatures

I will put into my dream
A land of sweets and candy
I will be the queen
Have a hamster to play with

My dream is fashioned from
Candyfloss clouds that start moving
When you take one out of them

I shall dive into my dream
It was as if it was a swimming pool of dreams.

Emilia Godding (8)
Jennett's Park CE Primary School, Bracknell

The Magic Dream

I will put into my dream...
The wonders of outer space
A world of stationary
A dirty underground house

I will put into my dream...
Crying clouds with tears plopping to the ground
A world of Smiggle that always smelt lovely
A chocolate swimming pool that had strawberries
floating around

I will put into my dream...
A happy extended life
The inside of Mars
The inside of a pencil case

I will put into my dream...
A shimmering lake
A train track made of noodles
A gingerbread house

My dream will be fashioned of
Myself diving into the wonders of a dream

I shall dive into my dream
With springs on my shoes that are as bouncy as a
kangaroo.

Zoe Williams (9)
Jennett's Park CE Primary School, Bracknell

The Land Of Imagination

I will put into my dream...
An animal paradise made of gems and chocolate
When it's night, look up because it will be beautiful
Each star has a different colour and they
shine like gold

I will put into my dream...
A world where every day is happy and full of rainbows
and rainbow love
Where no one gets hurt or injured

I will put into my dream...
A land where money doesn't exist and everyone is kind

I will put into my dream...
A world made of diamond that's as beautiful as a rose

I will put into my dream...
A land where snowflakes dance beautifully and turn
into a fairy

I will put into my dream...
A world full of love and hope.

Lola O'Neill (8)
Jennett's Park CE Primary School, Bracknell

The Magic Dream

I will put into my dream...
Warm hugs from a kind family
The magic of a glistening rainbow
The galloping of a unicorn

I will put into my dream...
The splash of a mermaid's tail
A roar of a lion
And the softness of a teddy bear

I will put into my dream...
The dancing of snowflakes
The dazzling of the sun
And the sparkle of the moon

I will fashion my dream...
A fantasy land of Lego
With a mouth-watering, everlasting chocolate fountain
And bowls made of strawberry laces

I will fly dive into my dream...
Landing in the past on to a cotton candy cloud
Then jump onto glowing jars of memories.

Lily Jane Mansell (8)
Jennett's Park CE Primary School, Bracknell

The Magic Box Of Dreams

I will put into my dream
The natter of humans talking to animals
The invisible people having fun at all times
The luxury mansion with the brownest chocolate pool

I will put into my dream
The sound of rattlesnakes
The drip of a tap left on
The boom of TNT blowing up

I will put into my dream
A diamond clapping at a birthday party
The glitter dazzling on the piece of art

I will put into my dream
The Coca-Cola as brown as a bear rolling in mud
The light as white as a polar bear rolling in snow

I will fly on a unicorn over my dream
And look at everything I have done in the past.

Tyler Chaplin (8)
Jennett's Park CE Primary School, Bracknell

Dreams

I will put into my dream...
Danielle, Jamie and I, playing rugby against demons
and we win

I will put into my dream...
Danielle, Jamie and I getting chased by a baby snow
leopard and eventually it becomes Danielle's pet
The top of my dream is encrusted with gems, the
bottom with spikes chiming and dinging

I will put into my dream...
Being a famous footballer and playing in FIFA

I will put into my dream...
Me and Elliot meeting James Bond and he taught us
how to make our guns spit out bullets

I walk my dream every night but in the day it cannot be
found as if it had disappeared.

Ethan Duggin (8)
Jennett's Park CE Primary School, Bracknell

The Magic Dream

I will put into my dream...
A gingerbread house with white puffs of smoke
Green fondant icing sprouting outside
Marshmallow pavements high and mighty

I will put into my dream...
A dragon roaring and shooting out fire
Ice-cold cages holding mythical creatures
The dragon flying

I will put into my dream...
Stationery made shops
Chocolate streets with a caramel fountain
Pancake clouds

I will put into my dream...
A woof of a dog
A miaow of a cat
A squeak of a mouse
And a purr of a lion

My dream will be fashioned from
A land of magical magic.

Emma Kemp (8)
Jennett's Park CE Primary School, Bracknell

My World Of Dream

I will put into my dream...
A unicorn with burger powers
And a sun that smiles every day

I will put into my dream...
A candy land with popping popcorn
and candyfloss clouds
And boys and girls as gummy bears

I will put into my dream...
A monkey that works for you and it can run as fast
as a car
And everyone is as happy as an excited puppy

I will put into my dream...
Money that grows on trees, so poor people can get it
And friends turn family

I will put into my dream...
A school of rainbow
Magic powers that I have

My dream is big!

Helena Jewell (9)
Jennett's Park CE Primary School, Bracknell

My Magic Dream

I will put in my dream...
A superhero with spectacular powers
A pirate having the best time of his life
A builder building a wizard school

I will put in my dream...
A dragon breathing toasty warm fire
An athlete running fifty miles
A twenty-five foot tall spider stomping on houses

I will put in my dream...
An astronaut in space discovering real planets
A famous footballer scoring fifty goals
A unicorn admiring herself in the mirror

I will put in my dream...
A clown playing tricks on everyone
A teacher making children work hard
A wizard putting spells on a child.

Laila Rose Frank-Gore (8)
Jennett's Park CE Primary School, Bracknell

The Magic Dream

I will put into my dream
Flying to the moon on a unicorn
The brick of a fairy's castle
A good spider with a magical horn

I will put into my dream
A very happy life for everyone
People would fly with wings
Stardust from a shooting star

I will put into my dream
The fire from a dragon
A mad world of smiggle
Harry Potter Warner Bros studios

I will put into my dream
Shrimps from Cornwall
A candy house with crisps for the roof
And a Coca Cola bottle for the chimney

I will fashion my dream from
Candyfloss that melts as quickly as ice cream.

Mia Perillo (8)
Jennett's Park CE Primary School, Bracknell

Dreaming Football

Once upon a dream there was a football player, better than ever, called Leon Frank-Gore, very clever
Shooting goals, beautiful goals, making the
crowd go, 'Woohoo!'
Midfield attack, outstanding midfield attack, making the crowd go, 'How did he do that?'
Left wing, amazing left wing, making the crowd go, 'I want to be a left wing!'
Right wing, marvellous right wing, making the crowd go, 'I want to be a right wing!'
Defence, incredible defence, making the crowd go, 'Good defence!'
Good keeping, whopping goalkeeping, making the crowd go, 'Great goalkeeping!'

Leon Charles Frank-Gore (8)
Jennett's Park CE Primary School, Bracknell

Dreams

I will put into my dreams
A ginormous quiche trap
So villains do not escape from prison

I will put into my dreams
The sound of cannons on pirate ships

I will put into my dreams
The crashing and splashing of
The Great Barrier reef
Onto the moon and then
There will be floating fish

I will put into my dreams
A nightmare
There was a talking dummy
And kept on calling everyone Papa

I will put into my dreams
Me surfing on a missile

I will put into my dreams
Two year olds driving cars.

Anthony Lopez (8)
Jennett's Park CE Primary School, Bracknell

Magic Dream

I will put into my dream
The graceful smiles of rainbows
Cats purring proudly
Fish splashing

I will put into my dream
Snow dancing elegantly
Wind whooshing
Clouds crying

I will put into my dream
The sun giggling happily
Pencils writing
Pencils and pens colouring

I will put into my dream
The big bang in outer space
And a happy life
With a brush to brush out the badness

My dream is fashioned out of a candy land

I float in my dream desperate to see the underworld.

Aaryaa Awasthi (9)
Jennett's Park CE Primary School, Bracknell

The Magic Dream

I will put into my dream
Some fairy flutter
The queen of chocolate
Fairies made of sweets

I will put into my dream
An ice seating rainbow
Candyland of candyfloss
To be on chocolate clouds

I will put into my dream
Everything that is smiggle
With a galloping Kraken
And Harry Potter's wand

I will put into my dream
An eagle flying to the moon
To be in the midnight gang
And dancing prince tapping

My dream will be fashioned from candyfloss
I shall sprint into my dream as fast as a cheetah.

Priscilla Abankwa (8)
Jennett's Park CE Primary School, Bracknell

The World's Best Dream

I will put into my dream
Wonderful cheese pizzas
Crazy pepperoni people
Cheese is on the floor

I will put into my dream
Awesome rainbow football
Then I play at Anfield and score

I will put into my dream
Shiny diamonds, as shiny as the sun
The world is gems
People are whizzing

I will put into my dream
Jumping gummy bears
Yummy sweets

I will put into my dream
Fizzing Coke
And lemonade everywhere

I will not put in my dream
Fire dragons chasing me
Slithering snakes.

Jude Richard-James Carswell (9)
Jennett's Park CE Primary School, Bracknell

The Magic Dream

I will put into my dream...
The whoosh of a dragon flying past a bunch of leaves
The rocket blasting behind space to
explore imaginary worlds
I will go to the future to see the upside-down world

I will put into my dream...
The horizon of paradise sea
To go into a private jet to lands never seen

My dream box is made of
special items that have never been found before
With stars on each corner of the box
and on the side is chocolate

I will leap in my dream
I will surf into my dream
I will flip into my dream.

Joshua McCarthy (9)
Jennett's Park CE Primary School, Bracknell

The Magic Dream

I will put into my dream
The fluffy marshmallow clouds floating above us
In the twinkling night sky.

I will put into my dream
Snow dancing from the perfect clouds
And the snow is trickling down like a shooting star.

I will put into my dream
The candyfloss trees dancing around
The mouth-watering chocolate sea.

I will put into my dream
A shiny fish diving in and out of the sea
A blackbird singing a wonderful song
Long grass swaying in the breeze.

Sienna Mulholland (8)
Jennett's Park CE Primary School, Bracknell

Disaster Dream

D ead bodies lying around the writer's house
I nside the house it was crawling with the mouse
S eeing a book I opened it to the first page
A nd before I knew it I was trapped in a cage
S piders' den that's where I am
T hey might fry me in a human-sized pan
E ating the fly off the webs
R ight, that's it, I was in a cage of webs.

D isgusted, I moved the webs to the side
R unning from spiders I could feel I had pride
E xplosion right ahead of me
A t least five miles away
M y eyes opened, it was only a dream.

Karthini Sharma (10)
Kennet Valley Primary School, Reading

Imagination

Soaring above the clouds near the snowy mountains
The fiery sun sets below the emerald
horizon behind me
Happiness is swelling like a balloon inside me
But when I think it's going so well
And unlit and gloomy fog swirls around me
I stop abruptly in mid-air
In dark and leathery and is unmistakable
Those orange eyes like fire glow eerily
He growls with fury
He snatches me up with unmistakable force
I am on his back, clutching for dear life
Oh help, there's a dragon coming to imprison me
He takes me to his lair
It's a dark void in a nutshell
I can only make out his slaves, sickly green lizards
Oh dragon, have mercy, I plea
He pays no notice
Leering at me, he shows his needle-sharp teeth
He prepares to pounce
I close my eyes in dread, waiting for sudden death
Suddenly I feel the comfort of my bed

Relief washes over me like washing up water over the gleaming plates
It was just my imagination gone wild.

Heidi Lewis (10)
Kennet Valley Primary School, Reading

Green Dragon

G rowing quickly, my fear reminds me, I'm scared of dragons

R acing away, I run from the dragon

E ventually I get away then I found him again

E xhausted, I ran in circles away from my enemy

N ever going to get away from the dragon.

D riving through the muddy woods on a dark, dark day

R iding away on a dragon trying to kill me

A bout to rip me guts out

G oing to hurt me and destroy the ghostly woods

O ne more step and I am dead

N o one can save me now

S uperheroes glide down and save me, I was wrong, someone did save me.

Sienna Cluderay (10)

Kennet Valley Primary School, Reading

Nightmare In The Station

Imagine
The sun fades on the horizon
The tear going *drip, drop, drip*, as it goes to the
grounds of the floor
to make her eyes

Imagine
The smoothness of her hair in the daylight
The cautious creep that she takes every second
To make her hair

Imagine
The nippiness of her body
The coldness as a sinister heart like an ice cube
To make her heart

Imagine
The clatter of her teeth shivering in the
cold winter wonderland
The quivering teeth are as cold as liquid nitrogen.

Norah Cyril (10)
Kennet Valley Primary School, Reading

Midnight Corner

As the midnight moon shines on my feet
I see darkness flicker in front of me
Suddenly, out of the dark, damp alleyway
My ears hear the pitter-patter of giant green feet
Heart beating, black fog soars around me
The dancing grass swaying left and right
Died when the roar of a mysterious beast filled the air.

I sensed the ground below shake and tremble
Thoughts whizzing around my head
I see his blood-red beady eyes, ready to devour me
However, my eyes automatically closed
There, my body lay in bed, untouched.

Cody Sanders (10)
Kennet Valley Primary School, Reading

The Tall, Gangly Figure

'Save me,' I cry, thoughts swirling through my head
My heart pounding, I tiptoe instead
Down the dark, narrow alley I hear a pitter-patter
I whip around to see a man in tatters
A tall, gangly shadow towers above
A hand reaches towards me, I see a glove
Thick, musty air slaps my face
I peek around to see not a single trace
The glow of eerie eyes had disappeared
I bolt up awake, sitting in bed
My heart thudding yet I was safe in my
own lovely cottage
It had just been a dream, a very unpleasant dream.

Naeema Chowdhury (10)
Kennet Valley Primary School, Reading

In The Clouds

Imagine
The soft marshmallow lifting me out of my
warm, cosy bed
Flying above the emerald horizon
My heart pounding as we fly higher
I look down and see a dragon circling below me
The trees dancing in the breeze as we go past.

Imagine
The strange look on my face as a wizard
appears beside me
Clouds speaking in a gentle, calm voice
A fairy fluttering above my head.

Imagine
Falling from such a height
And landing back safe and sound in my bed
What an adventure.

Mia Elisa Dell (9)
Kennet Valley Primary School, Reading

My Worst Fear

N ever will I take one step into the woods again

I magine a dragon chasing you on a stormy night

G rabbing my wrists, please let me go!

H ave you felt this sad and worried

T *hud...* I hear falling

M y worst fear came to life. Oh no, I think it might be him

A fter I hear the feet of roaring dragons

R ight there a flash of light in the distance

E erie eyes staring into my soul

S uddenly I appear in my bed, nothing to be worried about or do I...?

Amber Dixon (9)
Kennet Valley Primary School, Reading

Nightmare In The Woods

Skipping and stepping in the dark, misty woods
Stepping on the crunchy leaves
Crunch, crunch, crunch with my best friend
I can see incy wincy spiders
My teacher turning into a zombie
I can see lights flickering about the sky

My teacher was coming to get me
The spiders were crawling over me
Wizards came to save me
They put a spell on them
Whoosh, they are all gone

Wizards took me to Wizard Land
But that's not all...

Avie Alcock (9)
Kennet Valley Primary School, Reading

The Land Of Fire-Breathing Dragons

Getting lost in a land of dragons
I spot dragons storming around
I hear the crispness of dragons stomping on leaves
My heart was beating as fast as a cheetah
I smell burning smoke tingling through my nostrils
Fossils of dragons under the soil
Dragons flying over a dark and misty bridge
I scurry beneath them only to get the firing line
of their breath!
The dragon was about to burn me
But then I suddenly woke up in shock
I was so happy it was just a dream.

Christina Paul (9)
Kennet Valley Primary School, Reading

Run For Your Life!

It was a blur
Sprinting towards me as fast as a cheetah
A red wig bobbing up and down
Then *whoosh*, I found myself flying in the night sky
Twinkling stars gazing at me
I saw neon colours in the colour of my eye
Superheroes, I worked it out
I was flying with them
All of a sudden I was burning hot
Small, black pupils staring into my eyes
Closer it comes
Then warm in my bed
Thank goodness, it was only a nightmare.

Olivia Webb (10)
Kennet Valley Primary School, Reading

In The Alley

Slowly, silently walking down an alley,
The wind blowing a scary melody,
Lampposts flickering in the night sky,
Monsters hiding in the dark shadows.

The bushes moving like Dementors searching
for your soul,
Chuckles, chuckles wherever I go,
What was that,
No one knows.

A black creature chasing me,
His face was red as can be,
Out of the alley,
Into the valley.

Daniel Birose (10)
Kennet Valley Primary School, Reading

Dreaming

U nder the swishing and swirling tree
N earby, the flowing river, on top of the white fluffy clouds
I n the dark, gloomy cave I heard a *thud!*
C reaking on the hard falling rocks
O ne spider dropped down, it scared me, I jumped out of my skin
R un someone is coming!
N ever, never go back again!

Kirstie Bates (9)
Kennet Valley Primary School, Reading

Mysterious Creature

D arting across the sky, I see an island
R ight when I land, I knew it was a bad idea
A round the corner I see an approaching shadow
G etting closer I see the creature
O range scales and blue eyes
N ostrils that can smell you seven miles away.

Casper Jennings (9)
Kennet Valley Primary School, Reading

Untitled

One late, dark night walking through the woods
Listening to every sound
When suddenly I spied a clown up a tree
I started to run as fast as I could
Felt like I was drowning, couldn't breathe
I was lifted up
So relieved that Flappy saved me
My pet dragon.

Jack Robert Bayliss (9)
Kennet Valley Primary School, Reading

The Dream Fairy

A fluttering fairy comes at night
Her hair is blonde, her eyes are bright
She has this dazzling delicate smile
That makes you want to sleep a while!

She has a little golden wand
That sprinkles golden fairy dust
She sends you into gusts of dreams
Where happiness spreads like the wind

The things that I see in my dreams
Are happy and pleasant all that can be
With pixies and unicorns galloping on
I feel this dream can never end

I see gullible goblins running wild
Magnificent mermaids swimming about
Preposterous pixies chanting curses
Nothing is better than this audacious paradise

This heavenly kingdom is an enthralling land
Full of mystery, magic and thrilling adventures
Pulling you towards the endless happiness
This cosmic country never ends
While the dream fairy sits and waves.

Tanvi Davuluri (11)
Marish Primary School, Slough

Candy Land Dream

The sweet smell of heaven is on its way
Gushing chocolate smoothie, waterfalls spray.
I am in this unknown world
Over the sweet candy cane hills I rolled.
The elegance was prettier than ever
Mr Candy, you are *ever* so clever.

'Let's go and get some candy!' exclaimed Yana
For it was such a tropical savannah.
I saw a magical unicorn
He was ever so red, so I called him Fire Scorn.
So on the way to the gummy kingdom
The candyfloss clouds a-twinkle.

Into the halls of wisdom
Yana was full of determinism.
Flabbergasted we were, to see the great Mr Candy
I bet he was the Spanish grandee.
'All we want is to get home, for 10 o'clock in sight!'
Well... goodnight!'
Off we teleported back home
Now we were alone...

Zara Amber Khan (11)
Marish Primary School, Slough

Unicorn

The unicorn with the long, white hair
It's beautiful and wild
Unicorns are beautiful
Just like a soft rainbow
I made a rainbow unicorn
We sailed across the sky
Its mane was bright and colourful
It sparkled shimmered and shone
Shooting rainbows around her
She flew to heaven to see her grand lord
How beautiful she was
Dressed up in a red, sparkling seas
The mare wore a golden coat and had a white tail
Her tail fell on the ground like a waterfall
Unicorns singing happily as the night fades away
They look at the lake to grab some fish
They are having dinner with delicious cupcakes
Diamonds on crowns are sparkling.

Hasini Pulavarthi (8)
Marish Primary School, Slough

Nightmare Or Not

D readful monsters chasing my wonderful unicorn and I am

R eally frightened, they are coming from all directions

E nthusiastically slobbering, longing to gobble me up

A ppearing from everywhere and surrounding me, what should I do?

M aybe they will spare me and have mercy on my unicorn

S uffering dreadfully from shivering frostbite

C an I survive this horrible situation

A re these monsters just a dream?

R unning won't help because they are as fast as lightning!

Y et I think something strange is going on - they are attacking my mouth-watering cupcake!

Druti Vasist (11)
Marish Primary School, Slough

Emerald Unicorn

E verything shimmers and sparkles
M umbling all around me
E ating multicoloured rainbows
R oaring rapidly like a lion
A t the pond I glare gloriously
L eaping speedily through the island
D eep in the crystals treasure lies.

U nder the sea fish are sly
N ever cry and you'll never lie
I 'll always repeat so don't be shy
C urious you'll be but that's not for me
O bviously I'll see you but just in a week
R apidly you crawl round the table
N ot talking rudely but joyfully.

Natalia Dudek (8)
Marish Primary School, Slough

Lost Dream!

The wind is howling furiously, *whoosh!*
Something shaking, lurking in the bush
Where am I
I'm so scared I could cry
The sky is a pitch-black cover
Take me back to my mother
A waterfall is leaking from my face
I begin to run at my fastest pace
This is my worst nightmare
It's really, really not fair
I begin to shudder, *brrr*
I think I heard a wolf, *grrr*
It's so cold I begin to shake
Slowly my eyes open, I'm awake
Oh my gosh, it was all fake
Now I'm safe and sound cosy in bed
Luckily it was just a dream made up in my head!

Naomi Nash (11)
Marish Primary School, Slough

Flying With Fairies

Bright orange sun rising high
From beyond dark blue mountains up to the sky
There comes the little fairies
Flapping their wings, dancing on berries
Peeking through the window
I signalled to a little fellow
The fairy flew forwards to say hello
I jumped out to follow
With no wings, how can I fly?
Fairies with pixie dust took me high
Holding my hands left and right
We dip and dive, fly and dance till the night
What fun it is to fly high
it is time to say goodbye
Hoping for another day with my fairy friends
Slept tight holding my teddy's hands.

Isha Pothineni (8)
Marish Primary School, Slough

The Future

As God blows the trumpet it's finally time
To take away bad mischief, to take away bad crime
The formal angels ring their golden bells
Nature flourishes, snails come out of their shells

The creatures scuttle out of their houses
People stop calling on their phones
Everyone has attention on the trumpets blow
The melody has a calm, sweet flow

God takes us up with a twist and a twirl
Heaven is beautiful, more lovely than a pearl
Everyone has liberty as happy as can be
This is how the future is going to be with me.

Unique Oluoha (7)
Marish Primary School, Slough

The Hula Flower Blooms!

There is a flower that blooms every year
So you better go with great care
If you want to see it bloom
You should reach there as soon.

The flower does a hula dance
And sways its leaves in the grass
When it dances it can make you laugh.

What would you do if you go to watch the show
It will be down the waterfall a bit low
The flower would like you to sing so it can dance
to the beat
You can make a skirt out of leaves and dance along on
both your feet.

Arshiya Gupta (7)
Marish Primary School, Slough

Miss Unicorn

Where are you Miss Unicorn
I didn't see you out back in the garden
I flew through wavy clouds
And then I got a bit stuck in one of them.

Your bright pink curly hair
And your multicoloured tail
That can be seen miles away
My mind forgets all the fears from today.

The clouds are fading
You must be close by
I hear your magical flying
And clearly see your eyes shine brightly in the sky
I knew you would be back tonight.

Chloe Corcoran (7)
Marish Primary School, Slough

I'm An Athlete

With speed like a swift
Always persevering
I disappear into the mist
'Go on Olympian! Keep endearing!'

Crowds are cheering
All surrounding me like sharks
Salty sweat oozing
'Go on Olympian! Do your tasks!'

Encouragement filing me deep within in
My pride is leisurely filling
It was a win!
'You did it Olympian! Now be rejoicing!'

Rithvick Dittakavi (10)
Marish Primary School, Slough

Football

Football is a nice game to play
Kick the ball how high you can
Play with your mum, play with your dad
Always be happy, never be sad
Play football all day long
You will stay healthy, fit and strong
Every day loved football, I bet
Look at the ball - it is in the net
Passing the ball, scoring the goals
Having fun, asking for more.

Bartlomiej Brandys (8)
Marish Primary School, Slough

My Football Dream

F ocus on the ball

O ver the crossbar, it may go

O r in the back of the net, hear the roar

T ackling is what we do

B ut don't get a yellow or two

A ll we want is to win

L osing would be a terrible sin

L oyal and loud, what a great crowd

Sam Hopkins (11)
Marish Primary School, Slough

My Carnivorous Tiger

My tiger is deep in sleep,
Dreaming of chases remembered,
His keen eyes are glinting and he dreams of sprinting,
Some boar will soon be dismembered.

I wish to actually have,
Oh please our own separate dreams!
When he says, 'I'll have a midnight feast.'
I'm telling you that's what he means.

If I eat anything,
That will give me just an ounce,
He jumps on me and eats me up,
In one gigantic pounce.

Oh no, he's eaten me up again,
I'm getting sick of this now,
I wish I could wallop out of here,
With one great big kapow!

Oh god, I'm awake, thank god for that,
No more Willy Nilly or Nelly,
Wait, it's odd in here, oh no my dream is true,
I'm right here in his belly!

Gabriel Alexander Addario-Prado (9)
Nas Thames Valley School, Reading

The Knight Quest

The dragon was guarding a hoard of gold,
He got woken by a brave knight.
He used the magic notebook to make comrades
And get ready for the fight.

He created the archer,
With fire arrows and a bow.
To shoot down the dragon's wings
And make him fly low.

The horseman and his brown and white horse,
Rides around the dragon with his lance.
The dragon's eyes go red
And the dragon does a dance.

The dragon kept on fighting,
The knights began to tire.
The archer ran out of arrows
And the dragon breathed out fire.

James Sandford (9)
Nas Thames Valley School, Reading

The Zombie Apocalypse

Our leader said, 'Let's defeat these zombies
In the abandoned city
But look out for some health
If you die it will be a pity.'

They walked to the park
And found some health packs
They saw some armoured zombies
They started to attack.

The battle was vicious
Lots of people got hurt
The men won the battle
The zombies were buried in dirt.

The city grew back again
They all celebrated
They all went back home
The city was gated.

Dominic Bell (9)
Nas Thames Valley School, Reading

Zombie Teacher

Our teacher said, 'Let's cut some trees
In the dangerous woods
but look out for zombies
They will start to pull on your hoodies.'

The teacher said, 'I will help cut the trees
The trees are wide and big
But watch out for bees.'

The children said, 'We smell a zombie
It smells mouldy
It's coming closer
And it looks all goldy!'

Daniel Van-Asperen (9)
Nas Thames Valley School, Reading

Island

On the island you can smell the salty sea
You can hear the swishing breeze
You can eat the tropical fruit
You can see the flying bees
On top of the high trees,
you can see the glimmering sea
The waves crashing together
The bright sunset is going down
Then the moonlight stays forever
You can eat the big, juicy coconuts.

On the golden sand you can see some feathers
You can build sandcastles
You can see some leather
In the sea you might find some treasure
You might find some gold
You might make necklaces
And sometimes the weather is cold.

The sun shines on you
It's like you're on stage
It feels amazing
It's like you're in a book on a page
When the weather gets hotter we all boil up

Then we go in the sea to freshen up
We have a lovely time
Then we have a picnic and drink with a cup.

Maggie Sinani (10)
Park Lane Primary School, Reading

Fairies' Wand Dream

F abulous wings that glide in the wind
A bsolutely beautiful
I n a short blue dress
R osy-red cheeks on a summer's day
I love her unicorn
E xcellent hearing, good for hunting
S weet melody that draws me in

W eird feeling up inside
A nd without notice, I wake up
N othing is bothering me but a steep hill that I'm trying to get up
D on't care it's morning

D ad asks me, 'What's up?'
'R eally bad dream,' I say
'E ggs for breakfast?' says Mum from the kitchen
A nd now my friend asks me, 'What's up?'
'M e,' I say, 'Really bad dream!'

Emily Hall (9)
Park Lane Primary School, Reading

A Note From A Horse

I am with two ponies
We go to a valley
We ask for food and the way
All the elephants agree
Enthusiastically
'You can have anything you want!' they say
Just then
Suddenly
A horrible horse appeared
'Hee, hee, hee!'
He grinned nastily
Dropped some paper then disappeared
I picked up the note
Nobody could read it
And so I threw it away
We said goodbye
I tried not to cry
And said, 'We'll be on our way.'

Sreevedha Bhuvaneshwaran (8)
Park Lane Primary School, Reading

If I Could Fly!

If I could fly, I would swerve in and out of
cotton candy clouds
If I could fly, I would glide through the foggy night sky
with dragons the size of helicopters
If I could fly, I would swoop over the rooftops of
Reading, like an eagle seeking its prey
If I could fly, I would watch the joy on children's faces
as they play in the parks below
If I could fly, I would soar gracefully through the wind
with beautiful, majestic unicorns.

Thomas Brooks (10)
Park Lane Primary School, Reading

The Moonlight

M arvellous, always shining brightly
O verall it's been a good light
O bviously the moon is bright
N othing can bother you when you are asleep
L ovely light to say goodnight
I magine being on the moon
G uiding you safely home
H ome will always be found by the moonlight
T ucked up in bed to say goodnight!

I dream to be living on the moon!

Leah Whittington (9)
Park Lane Primary School, Reading

My Favourite Food

I like to eat fairy cakes
When my mum bakes
I like them with sprinkles
And even with wrinkles!
I like to eat crumble
When my tum has a rumble
I like it with ice cream
And for tea it's a dream!
I like to eat pizza
Must be margarita
I like it with chips
Although it's bad for my hips!
And last but not least
Is a raspberry feast
On a bed of meringue
With a dollop of jam!

Talullah Mae Linger (8)
Park Lane Primary School, Reading

Opposite Land

I am alone in the darkness of the forest
I push a branch and...
Wow, there are flying Dodos and super speed worms
Oh, oh, and don't forget the rainbow glow worms that
transform into pink and purple tigers
I can't believe my day is coming to an end
Or I'll miss the ferry home to London
I wish I could stay forever
Oh, I wonder what my next adventure is...
Big Ben or a random opera house?

Emilie Homer (10)
Park Lane Primary School, Reading

The Candy Unicorn

I made a unicorn
Out of sweets
Bubblegum, humbugs and cream
She felt like a dream.

I rode her over the sea
She flew like a honeybee
Her chestnut Bambi eyes glistening at me
As I listened to the breeze.

I fell asleep on a marshmallow cloud
When I woke up
My unicorn was gone!
All of a sudden
My mum shouted,
'Ready for school?'

Emily Watkinson (10)
Park Lane Primary School, Reading

Christmas Is A Great Time

Christmas is a great time for caring and sharing
Christmas is a great time for happiness and joy

Christmas is coming!
Christmas is a great time for hanging up the stockings
with great smiley faces
Christmas is a great time for having a break

Christmas is here!
Hooray! Shout with joy and dance around the sitting
room because it is Christmas time!

Isabella Charlotte Moon (7)
Park Lane Primary School, Reading

Unicorn

A unicorn is fluffy
A unicorn can fly
A unicorn can fight
A unicorn is funny
A unicorn is funky
A unicorn can be fat
A unicorn can be flat.

Anya Thomas (9)
Park Lane Primary School, Reading

The Show Must Go On...

The male ballerina leapt down the street
With every leap he pointed his feet
There it was at the end of the road
The majestic theatre called 'The Toad'

He took the back entrance door
And found the dressing number four
Dressed in the colour beige
He decided it was time to take the stage

On the stage he danced about
And the amount of people there was
impossible to count
Next to enter the stage was Mr Box
But instead entering the stage was a giant fox

There was only one clear way to be a hero
By defeating the fox one million to zero
They settled it with a dance battle
Even though the stage started to rattle

There was one clear winner
Who had earned themselves dinner
It was Harry
Who had just beaten a giant fox named Barry.

Harry Weston (11)
St Peter's CE Middle School, Windsor

Where Am I?

Where am I, that a place as cold, dark and
lonely should exist?
Should a lion's heart stop beating, skin of stone
crumble and the greatest warrior surrender for this
Isn't a place where bravery can grow.
I'm blinded by the darkness, but I reach out to the
unwelcoming scent of dangerous bark,
This bark wanted to bite back, for I was an intruder in a
place I had no recognise.
Oh please, show me the way out I'm not
yet strong enough,
Run! Leave! Escape!
How?
The trees wailed louder than a storm's rage, as fast as
the wind could touch my skin.

Where am I, that no light may seek refuge, my bones
pillars of ice, raining like needles constantly
but no clouds?
There are no beasts here, but I hear the cries
of a predator,
Courage loses me in the darkness but now I must
hunt for it.
Show me the way out I'm not yet strong enough,
Blood begins to caress my veins with its warm touch,

Forgive me, but I seek home.
A place where fire burns as bright as the stars may
shine in the sky or as bright as the moon's mysterious
glow as it sails through the sky.
The trees whispered louder than an ocean's battle
against a lighthouse,
as fast as a tiger's hunger will carry it.

Where am I, that wind should bite my senses,
fog replaces the air I breathe and Mother Nature
abandons her child?
A spark? A flash? Is that light I see, fighting for me,
seeking me I seek it?
One foot moves forward, the other further, the next
further than the other.
This is how I'll escape darkness.
Clawing through the fog, trees may branch out
to stop me.
But I will light this forest like a phoenix
from grey ashes.
Show me the way out,
My heart connects to my mind as I become whole,
I have found myself and now I must find home.
The light becomes brighter with each step,
until light is all I see and I understand why I
must keep running.
The trees were as silent as a dream, as fast as hope
can reach you in the darkest of forests.

Charlie Drane (11)
St Peter's CE Middle School, Windsor

The Wondering World

Not my usual morning I say
Woke up before the sun was awake
I wonder how I get to school swiftly
I always thought vehicles drove quickly

Trying to pull out my boots for soccer
I found myself being absorbed by my locker!
Zooming down a tunnel of sound
I felt anxious and quite dumbfound

I landed with a loud *thud!*
Fortunately not in mud!
I scanned the area with a frown
Realising I was upside down

The ceiling was a vivid blue sky
The volcano sending spouts of lava that rise
A warm breeze and gentle heat
The soft sound of birds singing tweet

I could hear the soft bubbling of a stream
Sparkled like millions of diamonds that gleamed
The ominous land stretched as far as the eye could see
Bright red rhododendron scattered randomly

I felt this was a land of magic and peace
Until I saw a monstrous beast
Long, scaly wings sprouted from its shoulders
Enough strength to carry ten boulders

Snake's head at the end of its tail
The terrifying beast was anything but frail
Goggling yellow eyes on a demonic face
Huge, spiralling antennae erupted from its base

Lunging with a sudden surge of powers
He was soon over me like a tower
Barbed, spiky teeth ready to strike
I couldn't even run for my life!

'Wake up! Wake up!' my mother cried
I jolted awake as soon as she tried
I gave her a quick look of despise
And ran downstairs to her surprise.

Shrey Gala (10)
St Peter's CE Middle School, Windsor

In A Galaxy Far, Far Away

Places you haven't even imagined before,
In the place of the dream that's where I would want

Unicorns prancing in every direction,
With a rainbow coloured mist following
their every step,
Mini aliens, cute as a puppy, were a new creation,
This amazing land has been here every day and every
night and upon you it has crept,
It is screaming for you but all you need is to do is force
it out for just one night.

Beyond all this exquisite colourful
and spectacular land,
Is a boring, dull, disgusting and grey school,
This is a very cruel school with the headmistress named
Miss Trunchbull who should be banned
But all these innocent aliens have to deal with
this old troll

But this peculiar day, an old woman said she
was a teacher,
Was the one day with no Trunchbull
meaning no cruelty,
The adorable aliens didn't know this creature,
But this creature let them,

finally experienced fun at school and were eventually happy some even got to sow,
But of course fun must always end and that fun ended here the next day was cruelty once again,
These cunning aliens experimented fun wanting it to go on forever,
So during one lesson of creating potion they fashion a group named never,
They attacked Trunchbull and with pride and courage beat her forever, no more days of cruelty
were to come.

McKenzie Hoogers (11)
St Peter's CE Middle School, Windsor

Freaky Friday

It was on a Friday in May,
When I had a very freaky day.
Our class were working in food tech,
When our teacher said, 'Hang on a sec!'

She left the room in such a rush,
But soon came back with a mighty gush.
Bang! The door slammed shut and in she came,
But shockingly did not look the same!

She looked rather weird,
With her messy, green beard.
Three eyes on her face,
She looked like something from space!

Startle, scared, amazed but confused,
None of us knew what we should do!
As she began to simmer and bubble,
We knew we were in a lot of trouble.

Before we knew it she was out of the window,
Speeding to her ship, raging go, go, go!

The class were all as quiet as a mouse,
Everyone wished to get back to their house.
All of a sudden I opened my eyes,

And looked all around me in great surprise.
Here I was lying in my bed,
To my amazement, it was all in my head.

Me and my bed breathed a great big sigh,
It had all been a dream, we weren't going to die!

I can never quite see my teacher the same,
Even though she was never playing the game!

Holly Lewis (10)
St Peter's CE Middle School, Windsor

Fabulous Features Of Mythical Creatures

A dragon can
Breathe fire and
What he likes to do most
Is use this remarkable talent
To make himself plenty of toast.

Mermaids have fish tails
So can't walk at all
They're good at water polo
But suck at basketball.

Cyclops only has one eye
Which means he cannot wink
Every time he has one go
It turns into a blink.

Medusa's a grumpy woman
So best you'd leave her alone
She has snakes for hair
And can turn you into stone.

A Centaur is half-human
But has four legs like a horse

He doesn't neigh or eat hay
But loves sugar lumps of course.

It's not much fun being a troll
Living under a bridge
He hasn't got a TV, sofa, a bath or fridge.

The Hydra's got nine heads
Can you imagine that
Imagine how much it would cost
If every head needed a hat.

None of these creatures are real you know
They are all just pretend
There are lots of other mythical beasts
But for now it's the end.

Elena Mills (11)
St Peter's CE Middle School, Windsor

The Dream

I lay back in my comfy bed
Slowly falling asleep
I begin to feel something
Like a tickle on my feet

I hear irritating sounds
Then gently open my eyes
Is that a Minotaur?
Am I dead? Am I alive?

I must be dreaming
A giraffe with eight legs
This isn't funny
Surely I am dead

A majestic colourful unicorn
Strutted down the lane
This mustn't be true...
Am I insane?

Anyway, what was tickling my feet
Looks like they've left some treats
Oh, it must be them sly leprechauns
Stomping down the street

The sun was blue and square
The moon was red and small
Trees were swaying side to side
Standing dominating, proud and tall

The ground started to shake
The houses started to crumble
I started to feel awake...
I heard someone mumble

My sister threw some water
All over my face
I woke up in a puddle
What a big disgrace.

Lilianna Nhamburo (11)
St Peter's CE Middle School, Windsor

Dreamland, Dreamland

Legendary lizards at your feet
Flying goats at the mountain peak

Dreamland, Dreamland, all is magical
When you enter this world, the wildlife is mystical
From frogs with walking sticks, to snakes
whose home stinks
Pink bushes made from candyfloss, to bored trees
with memory loss

Dreamland, Dreamland, all is magical
When you enter this world, the wildlife is mystical
Every day the phrase cats and dogs
It comes in handy when it is related to
the miserable bog

Dreamland, Dreamland, all is magical
When you enter this world, the wildlife is mystical
Not all had been unrevealed
As you will see your dreams in the field

Dreamland, Dreamland, all is magical
When you enter this world, the wildlife is mystical

Adam Fodor Sfendla (10)
St Peter's CE Middle School, Windsor

My Shape-Shifting World

Otis, show yourself, guide me through the night.
Make your hand destroy this ether, and behold,
a wonderful sight.
Let your body shape-shift again to how I
perceive you now.
Nothing bold or fancy, just a guiding sound.
Now that you hear me, don't betray me, enlighten me,
play with me now!
For truly, I know that you will never ever let me down.
Shape-shifter, you bring back so many memories, all so
glorious from our past.
You would turn into a Panda, and teach me
Kung Fu arts.
But now I'm in this nightmare and I really am trapped.
'So, Otis, get me out of here and onto the right track!'
At last, you've finally saved me, from exploring too far.
I'm coming back to my senses.
'Oh!' I hear the alarm.

Arjun Bassi (11)
St Peter's CE Middle School, Windsor

Stars

There are stars in the night-time sky,
Shining like diamonds,
Way, way up high.

I feel the wind as I'm lying on the soft grass
against my face,
It's cold but calm,
A man running trying to pick up his pace.

I feel as if I'm in a dream,
It's so peaceful,
If I got woken up that would have been mean.

Suddenly all the stars start to fall,
I panic wondering what to do,
I run to get help at the mall!

My friend and I start to glue,
We quickly start to rush,
Now all the stars are in the sky, then I randomly saw a
cow, it went moo!

Then it all went black and I'm back in my room,
Confused what happened,
On my bed wondering what to do!

Isabelle Brett (10)
St Peter's CE Middle School, Windsor

The Monster

The monster as black as night
Reached down through my window
And gave me quite a fright
Crept up to me like my greatest foe
Reached down and grabbed my arm
And sneaked out of my house
But as I am very charmed
I got out of his grasp, like a mouse
The trees looked like they were alive
I was so scared, so scared I nearly cried
I saw someone, but I was hypnotised
Walking into the unknown so, so sly
I could just about see a small cave
Every step I took I forgot more things
I saw so many, many slaves
Then I saw the smelly things
I was so close, so close
It picked me up and shoved one in its cage
I heard very scary singing
I wished, I wished that I could see my family again.

Jakob Howard-Real (10)
St Peter's CE Middle School, Windsor

Helping Hedgehog

Fox and Badger were in the woods one day
Not realising that they were going to save the day
It all started off where you could barely see
And that's when we saw the hedgehog under the tree
Was he asleep? Or was he unwell?
Fox and Badger just could not tell
As they went closer Hedgehog stirred and said,
'It's almost hibernation and I fear I could end up dead
I need to get to the hedgehog hospital soon
Before the end of the afternoon.'
They took him in the ambulance with
Fieldmouse the nurse
Who said, 'Don't worry, soon you won't
be feeling worse.'
The next day when Hedgehog was better
He went to hibernate and found a letter
But that is another story to be told.

Holly Alden (9)
St Peter's CE Middle School, Windsor

My Dream Life With A Twist

I live in a dream house
Where you can't hear a mouse
It has a pool
With a lovely hall
And also a lovely floor
But do you hear a *splash?*
Because someone's in the pool
Like Caleb, Lydia and I
But Portugal is as hot as a trip to the sun
And we just bought it
Then I heard a knock
And it sounds like Bang*! Bang!*
So I opened the door
And the person ran on the floor
And it is the queen
So I said, 'What are you doing?'
And she said,
'I am here to get away
From the swarm of the group.'
So I tell my mum and dad
And they say,
'What? she can stay for a bit.'
So she did.

Bo Isabel Sampson (10)
St Peter's CE Middle School, Windsor

Wonder

Wondering where you are
In a clueless dream
Or if you are in a wonderland
Beautiful green lands
Going through the lands
Full with wildlife

Big, loud sounds
With big vibrations
A dinosaur
Coming to me
With a bang
I go to hide
Within a cave
Spiders hanging
Looking hungry
There it is
The dinosaur starving
Wanting to kill

Then *crunch*, the dinosaur's head on the floor
Pouring blood everywhere

A shining creature
Wanders by

I'm terrified how the dinosaur died
What could it be
It wanders by
With a shine
Then with a surprise
Was a giant flying man.

Ewan Moore (11)
St Peter's CE Middle School, Windsor

The Tale Of The Shimada Brothers

There was once a time,
A time where two dragon brothers lived,
But they fought over who could lead to be fine,
So they battled until,
The brother Genji lost all will,
He fell to the ground causing a great tremor,
Hanzo had triumphed,
But when he realised what he'd done,
He knew he could not go on,
Then he met a man who asked why he
was so distraught,
And then the brother thought,
He suddenly understood and asked the man his name,
But the man was gone,
Hanzo knew this was a sign,
That this man came at the right time,
For Hanzo knew his brother was there,
He and his brother had made peace,
And ruled the land together!

Alec Collins (11)
St Peter's CE Middle School, Windsor

Sonnet Poem, The Wildlife!

Creeping and cheating, the lion stalks his prey
Sprinting and leaping, the scared prey runs
Without his catch, the lion is left astray
With no success the deed has not been done
As the night is upon us the leopard is on the prowl
The small impala hears his loud prints
As he creeps up on his prey, there is a loud growl
In a big dash, he starts his sprints
As he gets his catch he sits down to eat
Ripping and tearing through the thick meat
With his meal at his feet
Finishing the meal he thought what a treat
Oh I wish it could be another day
Oh I wish I could catch more prey
Hope all my dreams come true!

Georgia Van Der Brugge (11)
St Peter's CE Middle School, Windsor

Bruce

There once was a moose called Bruce
Who thought he was really a goose
'Honk, honk,' he would say
His friends laughed and walked away
He wished he lived in Madagascar
But he lived in North America
The beautiful mountains didn't please
He didn't want fur with the occasional flea
He wanted a bright orange beak and feathers
Webbed feet would be good in a variety of weathers
Bruce wanted to fly
So high in the sky
See the world, what was it like
He was bored of the woods and taking a hike
So slow and heavy, poor old Bruce
At least he could still dream of being a goose.

Millie Edwards (9)
St Peter's CE Middle School, Windsor

The Forbidden Forest

I see purple clouds
That remind me of clowns
I realise it's smoke, so I give it a poke
And then let it be as I spot a tree
I find out it is a forest as big as can be
I walk in the wood
Looking for food
But I see a tree
And it smiled at me
I say, 'Why hello Mr Tree.'
I turn around and see a monster munching a
giant fat bee
The monster is still hungry, he does not like that bee
He wants something juicy and tasty like me
I run away fast and feel like a rocket that's
about to blast!
I close my eyes as I am scared
But when I open them, I am back in my bed.

Thomas Sielski (11)
St Peter's CE Middle School, Windsor

Inspiring Moments

I looked into the pearl ice water for inspiration
I saw myself in a galaxy far from here
It was just me thinking this could be my reputation
Suddenly I heard a gunshot that seemed very near
I looked all around me and realised I was
I that galaxy running that race
My pounding heart was burning up inside me
This was it, my reputation or career
I was holding the gleaming gold trophy
With a wide grin on my face
I knew I had run and won the race

The host of the championships exclaimed,
'Dreams really do come true my dear!'

Ellie Breach (10)
St Peter's CE Middle School, Windsor

In The Lost Forest

I had a dream
About me in a lost forest
With my footsteps crunching and echo on the floor
As the wind sung its chorus
Voices went around my head
With the stars dancing in the night sky
But when I halted
A figure passed by
Knew what the figure was
But not the figure's face
I went to look for it
Like a detective on its case
Screams nearby were noted
Which haunted me as I speak
Then from the corner of my eye
The figure was there drinking from a creek
I stared at it for a while
Then it turned around

John Valdez (10)
St Peter's CE Middle School, Windsor

Things That Scare Me In A Dream!

S wirling sea and tidal waves crashing round my
battered body and I'm drowning, drowning,
drowning
C reepy castle with cobwebs and creaky floorboards
and I am hiding, hiding, hiding
A nimals with vicious teeth and sharp claws are
chasing me through a dark, dark forest and I'm
running, running, running
R ocketing off a knife-edge cliff, in a speeding,
speeding car because there is a woman driving, I
am falling, falling, falling
Y ou then always wake up and never remember a
thing, I get up and I'm happy, happy, happy!

Harry O'Shaughnessy (10)
St Peter's CE Middle School, Windsor

The Annoying Worm

The wardrobe was vibrating left and right
It shook up and down and it gave me a fright
I saw this figure bouncing off the walls, as bright as
a light bulb
Making everything else look small
Yapping and yapping, I could barely sleep
I could see Dad drive off in his new Jeep
Mum came in wondering, what's all the noise
I decided to hide under all of my toys
Shutting my eyes falling asleep
The annoying worm disappeared in the deep
I woke up the next morning as tired as can be
I told my family but no one believed me!

Leonna Nhamburo (11)
St Peter's CE Middle School, Windsor

The Earth Frog

Lounging on a cosy sofa
Playing with my serum
Patting my pet otter
Whilst spilling my complicated serum

The carpet bubbled, boomed and banged
I sat there with a frown
It morphed into blobby skin
All ghastly, slimy and brown

It was like a slimy rock
Dancing in the midnight sky
The slimy blob got sunburn
With a croak and said, 'Goodbye!'

My toad had green, dead eyes
And a very rocky back
His favourite snack in the Milky Way
As Mars is a bit too small.

Seth Thomson (10)
St Peter's CE Middle School, Windsor

Me And The Spirits

In the bowels of the museum, 12 o'clock sharp
Silently in the gloomy fog I walked forward
unknowing what to find
Peeking in the corridors forward and behind

Opening the doors the mist danced around
I spot the most wondrous sound
Uh-oh! I found a ghost
At first it was sorry but I scared it the most
Jumping in joy I pushed the lever
Knowing I just released my worst fear

Kicking and banging
My container gave in
You will never find out what is within.

Obi Ijeomah (10)
St Peter's CE Middle School, Windsor

The Wind Wolf

It was time for bed
When I said
Goodnight

Howling like the wolf it is
Running, I had spilt some tears
The wind wolf was back again

Growling, howling, the wind wolf ran
Faster and faster I jumped into a van
Will the wind wolf catch me?

Faster and faster the wind wolf flew
I was stuck on the spot like super glue
I was cornered by the wind wolf

Suddenly I opened my eyes, to see a great surprise
It was all a dream.

Harrison Wingrove (10)
St Peter's CE Middle School, Windsor

Australian Dream

I woke up in a taxi
Asked my mum, 'Where are we?'
Then we pulled up at a house
And I saw my cousin's mouse
That's when I realised we were in Australia
In went our suitcases with all our paraphernalia
Then I saw my cousin's mouse on the floor
I opened the door and there was more
I told my cousin to put them in their cage
And that's when I saw the rest of my family outside
under the shade
Then I heard a splash and I realised it was
Milo and Buff.

Eloise Hall (10)
St Peter's CE Middle School, Windsor

Famous

F retting to look good enough I don't know what to wear

A limo pulled up at my big black door and it gave me a scare

M ust I go, I won't know what to say I'll look really stupid in front of Beyoncé

O range was the theme, the room was like a pumpkin the only way in was by using your thumbprint

U nexpectedly Beyoncé won the award, she thanked me, OMG!

S tepping up I shut my eyes tight to wake up in my bed cold at night.

Liberty Groves (11)
St Peter's CE Middle School, Windsor

Dreamland

Where everything is upside-down
Far, far away from Earth
In a land as soft as a pillow
Planes fly upside down
Cars drive on their roofs

A monster, Mr Monster
Flying through the sky
Dropping all his mud in Dreamland
'Get out,' I say to the monster

Dreamland is a mess now
What do I do, what do I do now?
Oh that monster, he is really annoying
The magic jar waved at me
Goodbye Dreamland.

Oliver Wright (11)
St Peter's CE Middle School, Windsor

Scared Of The Dark!

I'm scared of the dark
I don't know where I am
But I want to get out of here
I see spooky skeletons with face paint
Which remind me of the day of the dead
And some multicoloured ghosts coming out of nowhere
I ran swiftly like a hare getting eaten by its predator
My worst fear is realised - it's a spooky, scary clown
Suddenly I felt like a zombie grabbed my leg
And then
Thud!
It was cat who grabbed my leg!

Roxanne Rejnisz (10)
St Peter's CE Middle School, Windsor

Guinea Pigs

G oing to sleep one night
U sually they get a fright
I n the middle of going to sleep
N ever in the day
E ach of the piggies
A lways cuddle up to each other.

P etrified that they had no food
I n their panic and in a bad mood
G ot to the fridge, but couldn't reach any food then...
S urprise! It was a dream and Ben fed them their favourite! Spinach!

Ben Pleace (10)
St Peter's CE Middle School, Windsor

Imagine

As I dreamed
My parents arrived
The sun beamed
And our imagination ran wild

My dad imagined snow
And it snow
My mum imagined a spa dome
And I appeared

I imagined puppies and kittens
Thousands appeared
It was cold so we got some mittens
My parents then imagines the Northern Lights

How beautiful it was
But my dad created gas!
I sadly woke up with a *bang!*

Charlotte Roberts (10)
St Peter's CE Middle School, Windsor

Walking On Clouds

I had a dream
A song to sing
A tale to tell
And ring my bell

As the morning woke
I thought this is a joke
How can this be?
I am now free!

No more tears
Or having any fears
Now I can walk
And never stop to talk

I'm dancing on the moon
As my friends sleep in their room
I can't wait for them to wake
And walk me down the lake

Joshua Ernest Claassen (10)
St Peter's CE Middle School, Windsor

At Night...

A twinkling star with all his might
T he sun has hidden with a fight

N o stand or whisper around
I take a step forwards as gentle as can be
G lancing left and right, while the freedom is outside
H ow will I sleep without a face, or I'm missing a loving grace
T he night has ended, so have I, so now let's say goodnight and sleep tight.

Amani Mahamud (11)
St Peter's CE Middle School, Windsor

The Lucid Dream

My house is a white void if you could see
All like before observe carefully
Although it is blank but think for a while
All will be changed with a wink and a smile
Bang, there's a dragon sleeping in a cave
There's a damsel in distress I have to save
It can't last forever, goodbye I have to wave
I wish the end was a little late
That's another 24 hours to wait.

Jamie Haydock-Wilson (11)
St Peter's CE Middle School, Windsor

Friends

Making a million friends is not a miracle
The miracle is to make a friend who will stand by you
When millions are against you
Friendship means understanding, not agreement
It means forgiveness, not forgetting
It means the memories last even if contact is lost.

F irst
R elation
I n
E arth, which
N ever
D ies...

Joshua Williams (10)
St Peter's CE Middle School, Windsor

The Battle

If you wanna know why
We're going really high
Zooming to the sky
We're going on a trip
In our cosmic battleship
And when we get to the right height
We shall fight the aliens!
With our lasers and our shields
In the galactic battlefields!
But we shall always fight
When we have the light
Of hope and glory
If the battle doesn't get too gory.

Angus Padwick (11)
St Peter's CE Middle School, Windsor

The Creepy House

I walked into the creepy house
I feel kinda sleepy
In the house you could hear a mouse
I heard a creak from the door
As I tiptoe on the floor
I walked and saw a pool
As I walked through the hall
I heard a squeak, so I peeped through the door
On the floor there was a flood of blood
The blood was as red as a rose
I really hope
That this was just a joke.

Yasmina Patricia Tahiri (11)
St Peter's CE Middle School, Windsor

Monsters Under My Bed!

There are monsters under my bed
And I can't get them out of my head
They slither and prowl
Even if I howl

The moon glistens in the night
That's when the monsters come out to fight
They have beady eyes
Yet gigantic thighs

They're different colours
But still are brothers
I quiver in fear
Whenever they are near.

Katie Beale (11)
St Peter's CE Middle School, Windsor

The Flight Of The Roller Coaster

I knew this wasn't planned
Breaking from the roller coaster
My small carriage pelted up
Up, up, up
Higher and higher my carriage races off
Spinning
Then it plummeted
Down, down, down
Faster than any rocket ship
Bumpier than any road
Suddenly there was a *thump!*
I woke up startled
Only to find, I fell onto my bedroom floor!

Olivia Clark (11)
St Peter's CE Middle School, Windsor

Footballer

F irst sport of fairness

O n and off makes you want to cheer on

O n the pitch makes you want to pray together

T oday we will have lots of fun playing pass

B y the pitch having fun with your mates

A ll of us come together and play

L ose or win makes you want to kick about

L oser or winner still enjoy the game.

Madinah Khan (11)
St Peter's CE Middle School, Windsor

My School Promise

Each day I'll do my best
And I won't do any less
My work will always please me
And I won't accept a mess
I'll colour very carefully
My writing will be neat
And I will not be happy
Till my papers are complete
I'll always do my homework
And try my best on every test
I won't forget my promise
To do my very best.

Ellie-Mai Worthington (10)
St Peter's CE Middle School, Windsor

Football

F ootball is amazing
O bserved by all the fans
O bvious that it is the best sport in the world
T o play is my dream
B alance is needed when in goal
A ll the people in the world love it
L et's all sing love it, love it
L et's all have a laugh and enjoy the game.

Jay Stephen Moody (11)
St Peter's CE Middle School, Windsor

The Unknown World

I'm a lost boy
In a lost world
Killer clowns roam the street
Monsters at my feet
Creepy crawlies
Drooly dolls
Monsters at my feet scatter away
They lay down dead just to rest their head
Myself runs towards me
The monster has got me
I'm in tears, I'm dead
The monster has won

Joshua Gomes (11)
St Peter's CE Middle School, Windsor

A Wonderful Car Ride

As I sit in the car
I think I see a shooting star
I see a lamppost turn into a candy cane
As we drive down the lane
I look at my school clothes
Now there is a gown!
And my hair is silky brown
My car turns into a carriage
And now I'm a cabbage
All of a sudden it goes wrong!

Morgan O'Neill (11)
St Peter's CE Middle School, Windsor

The Mish Mash Monster

The Mish Mash Monster
Short and fat
Likes curry and pickles
And was a furry cat
When the terrible monster hears me scream
All he does is wink with ease
When he eats with his snout
He does a funny vicious pout!
All I did was shout and scream
All to realise it was just a dream!

Ria Martin (10)
St Peter's CE Middle School, Windsor

Volcano

V olley of roars right at the very top
O utstanding surfaces that look as though they are
going to pop
L ooking at the sea
C oming to the dock
A nd when it comes to the bay
N o drop of water makes it through the day
O n the volcano of decay.

Charles Keen (11)
St Peter's CE Middle School, Windsor

Pirates

P irates sail across the sea
I n boats that are quite rickety
R olling waves toss them about
A fter a whale opens his water spout
T reasure is a pirate's loot
E very pirate needs a boot
S ea sickness is a pirate's enemy.

Edith Armfield-Shepherd (11)
St Peter's CE Middle School, Windsor

Famous

F lashing lights everywhere
A bright red carpet waiting there
M illions of people all watching me
O ver the world for all to see
U p on the stage I am filled with pride
S aluting my fans with my family at my side.

Ben Puscy (11)
St Peter's CE Middle School, Windsor

Wizard

Mr Wizard make a monster
Write (dinosaur and monster)
With powers
With teaching

Mr Wizard
Write (dragons with clowns)
With royalty
And fame

Mr Wizard
You're epic.

Brandon McCulley (11)
St Peter's CE Middle School, Windsor

The Storm

The storm is fading, you must be close by
I can hear the jingle of your bell
And then through the clouds
I see your eyes shine
Tonight I know I'll sleep well.

Grace Williams (10)
St Peter's CE Middle School, Windsor

School Of Magic

I dream of magic
Potions and a friend
With adventures so fantastic
They seem to never end

I have magical powers
And attend a wizarding school
A castle that towers
It's a fact that it's cool

There are dragons and mandrakes
And flying broomsticks too
On the first day we get cakes
And a plate of food or two

We have wands and cats
Robes and broomsticks
We wear pointed hats
And my cat's name is Felix

My favourite teacher
Has a lazy eye
Teeth like a beaver
And a long black tie

It's time for my favourite class
Need to grab my broomstick
I'm hoping to scrape a pass
By flying super quick

As I make a smooth landing
I stop and look to see
All the teachers standing
Clapping and cheering for me

But at last my friends
As the morning nears
My fantastic dream ends
And I shed some tears

Aaliah Malik (10)
Willow Primary School, Slough

I Wish I Was A Dancer!

I wish I was a dancer
I could do floaty dance
I wish I was a dancer
So I could choose my own floaty dance
I wish I was a dancer
So I can add lots of new skills to my dance
And get carried away by the beats
I wish to be a dancer
So I could name my dance
'The Fun Sun' would be my dance
I wish I was a dancer
I wish I was a dancer

I wish... I wish... I wish
I was a dancer

Would I need some
Practise

I wish I was a dancer
So I could meet
And greet my dance
Friends

I wish I was a dancer
So I could be at the top
Brilliant dancers on my team

Ting! Ting! Ting!

Wait! Where am I?
I'm at home, that was
The loveliest dream I ever had

OMG, a ticket for dancers
To take an amazing audition
It seems I'm in my dream!

Kaaynat Anwar (9)
Willow Primary School, Slough

Football Star Me! (A Dream)

I dreamt a dream of a ball! A football!
I kicked here and there and everywhere
Everyone was cheering me, shouting out loud! 'Amin! Amin!'
My football was kicked high and low, I take it everywhere I go!
Into the net it went; a goal I scored, yippee!
I am so happy as can be, my football goes everywhere with me
I play it in the park, in my garden, my friend's home too
Oh we love to play and kick the football, high and low
Into the frame it goes, hits the crossbar! Penalties too!
Tackling here and everywhere and everyone

I just love my football
I kick it high
I kick it low
I take it everywhere I go!
Ah, me and my football
Off to sleep I go...

Raja Amin Khan (9)
Willow Primary School, Slough

Orphan Child

A poor little child at the age of eight
Who feels that he has no fate
His dad has passed on and his mother has gone away
Which leaves poor orphan child alone today
He is unhygienic but that's not his fault
He can't find food, shelter, clothes, so that brings him
to a halt
His life is bad but his dreaming is good
All the time he visits a place where his
mother last stood
There is no clean water but the only water he can
find holds parasites
He is never on a roller coaster of emotions only one
stands out to him
That emotion is sadness, he can't even remember the
places he's been.

Imaan Jalil (9)
Willow Primary School, Slough

Unicorn Dreams

U ntil I see
N othing can be
I t's your bright pink hair
C ome here, it's swishing in the air
O pening my present, a unicorn with multicoloured tail
R unning through the forest I turn pale
N othing in my sight

D reaming in bed, I hug myself tight
R aising my hand I take a glare
E ven though it was a dream, there is bright pink hair
A t my door there is a knock, butterflies in my tum
M aybe it's a unicorn! Only my mum
S aying to myself unicorn dream, goodnight magical
unicorn, I should go to sleep.

Muqaddas Kamran (9)
Willow Primary School, Slough

Nightmare Moon

The moon is a nightmare for me
It brings me ghastly dreams
I have imagined lightning and thunder
Striking the trees
They let all their anger to the trees
But the trees can't fight

The raindrops are turning into balls of frozen ice
They land with a *thump!*
I feel the souls of ghosts following me around
But I don't turn
When I hear the footsteps it feels like somebody
throttling me heart

Each and every night, when the
nightmare moon comes
I step in a dreamland of worries.

Skeena Zara Shah (9)
Willow Primary School, Slough

Famous!

F ighting for my future
A cting according to my plan
M arching on like a trooper
O utcome should be better than when I began
U nderstanding it will be hard work
S ecuring being famous and enjoying with a smirk.

Amirah Zamurad (9)
Willow Primary School, Slough

YoungWriters
Est.1991

YOUNG WRITERS INFORMATION

We hope you have enjoyed reading this book – and that you will continue to in the coming years.

If you're a young writer who enjoys reading and creative writing, or the parent of an enthusiastic poet or story writer, do visit our website **www.youngwriters.co.uk**. Here you will find free competitions, workshops and games, as well as recommended reads, a poetry glossary and our blog.

If you would like to order further copies of this book, or any of our other titles, then please give us a call or visit **www.youngwriters.co.uk**.

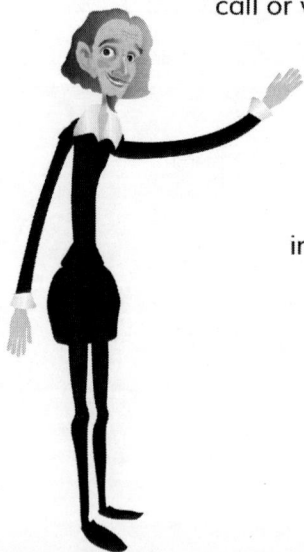

Young Writers
Remus House
Coltsfoot Drive
Peterborough
PE2 9BF
(01733) 890066
info@youngwriters.co.uk